Experiencing the Power of Life-Changing Faith

KAY ARTHUR
DAVID ARTHUR
PETE De LACY

HARVEST HOUSE PUBLISHERS
EUGENE, OREGON

Unless otherwise indicated, all Scripture quotations are from the New American Standard Bible®, © 1960, 1962, 1963, 1968, 1971, 1972, 1973, 1975, 1977, 1995 by The Lockman Foundation. Used by permission. (www.Lockman.org)

Verses marked KJV are from the King James Version of the Bible.

Cover by Koechel Peterson & Associates, Inc., Minneapolis, Minnesota

EXPERIENCING THE POWER OF LIFE-CHANGING FAITH
Copyright © 2011 by Precept Ministries International
Published by Harvest House Publishers
Eugene, Oregon 97402
www.harvesthousepublishers.com

Library of Congress Cataloging-in-Publication Data
  Arthur, Kay
  Experiencing the power of life-changing faith / Kay Arthur, David Arthur, and Pete De Lacy.
    p. cm.
  Includes bibliographical references.
  ISBN 978-0-7369-1273-0 (pbk.)
  ISBN 978-0-7369-4021-4 (eBook)
  1. Bible. N.T. Romans—Textbooks. I. Arthur, David II. De Lacy, Pete. III. Title.
  BS2665.55.A78 2011
  227'.1007—dc22

                                                              2010012467

Printed in the United States of America

14 15 16 17 18 19 / BP-SK / 11 10 9 8 7 6 5 4

CONTENTS

How to Get Started...

Reading directions is sometimes difficult and hardly ever enjoyable! Most often, people just want to get started. Only if all else fails will they read the instructions. We understand, but please don't approach this study that way. These brief instructions are a vital part of getting started on the right foot and will help you immensely.

FIRST

As you study Romans, you will need four things in addition to this book:

1. A Bible you are willing to mark in. The marking is essential. An ideal Bible for this purpose is *The New Inductive Study Bible (NISB)*. The *NISB* is in a single-column text format with large, easy-to-read type, which is ideal for marking. The margins of the text are wide and blank so you can take notes.

The *NISB* also has instructions for studying each book of the Bible, but it does not contain any commentary on the text, nor is it compiled from any theological stance. Its purpose is to teach you how to discern truth for yourself through the inductive method of study. Whichever Bible you use, just know you will need to mark in it, which brings us to the second item you will need...

2. A fine-point, four-color ballpoint pen or various colored fine-point pens you can use to write in your Bible. Office supply stores should have these.

3. Colored pencils or an eight-color leaded Pentel pencil.

4. A composition book or a notebook for working on your assignments and recording your insights.

SECOND

1. As you study Romans, you will be given specific instructions for each day's study. These should take you between 20 and 30 minutes a day, but if you spend more time than this, you will increase your intimacy with the Word of God and the God of the Word.

If you are doing this study in a class and you find the lessons too heavy, simply do what you can. To do a little is better than to do nothing. Don't be an all-or-nothing person when it comes to Bible study.

Remember, anytime you get into the Word of God, you enter into more intensive warfare with the devil (our enemy). Why? Every piece of the Christian's armor is related to the Word of God. And our one and only offensive weapon is the sword of the Spirit, which is the Word of God. The enemy wants you to have a dull sword. Don't cooperate! You don't have to!

2. As you read each passage in the Bible, train yourself to ask the "5 W's and an H": *who, what, when, where, why,* and *how*. Asking questions like these helps you see exactly what the Word of God is saying. When you interrogate the text with the 5 W's and an H, you ask questions like these:

> What is the chapter about?
>
> Who are the main characters?
>
> When does this event or teaching take place?
>
> Where does this happen?
>
> Why is this being done or said?
>
> How did it happen?

3. You will be given certain key words to mark throughout this study. This is the purpose of the colored pencils and the colored pens. If you will develop the habit of marking your Bible in this way, your study will be significantly more effective, and you will retain much more information.

Bible authors repeatedly use *key words* to convey their message to their readers. Certain key words will show up throughout Romans; others will be concentrated in specific chapters. When you mark a key word, also mark its synonyms (words that mean the same thing in the context) and any pronouns (*I, me, my, mine; you, your, yours; he, him, his; she, her, hers; it, its; we, us, our, ours; they, them, their, theirs...*) in the same way you marked the key word. Also, mark each word the same way in all of its forms (such as *judge, judges, judgment,* and *judging*). We will give you a few suggestions for ways to mark key words in your daily assignments.

You can use colors or symbols or a combination of colors and symbols to mark words for easy identification. However, colors are easier to distinguish than symbols. When we use symbols, we keep them very simple. For example, you could draw a red heart around the word *love* and shade the inside of the heart like this: **love**.

When we mark the members of the Godhead (which we do not always mark), we color each word yellow and mark *Father* with a purple triangle like this: **Father.** We mark *Son* this way: **Son** and *Holy Spirit* this way: **Spirit.**

Mark key words in a way that is easy for you to remember.

Devising a color-coding system for marking key words throughout your Bible will help you instantly see where a key word is used. To keep track of your key words, list them on a three-by-five card and mark them the way you mark them in your Bible. You can use this card as a bookmark.

4. A chart called ROMANS AT A GLANCE is included on page 121. As you complete your study of a chapter, record

the main theme of that chapter under the appropriate chapter number. The main theme of a chapter is what the chapter deals with the most. It may be a particular subject or teaching.

If you will fill out the ROMANS AT A GLANCE chart as you progress through the study, you will have a synopsis of Romans when you are finished. If you have a copy of *The New Inductive Study Bible,* you will find the same chart on page 1847. If you record your themes there, you will have them for a ready reference.

5. Always begin your study with prayer. As you do your part to handle the Word of God accurately, you must remember that the Bible is a divinely inspired book. The words that you are reading are truth, given to you by God so you can know Him and His ways more intimately. These truths are divinely revealed.

> For to us God revealed them through the Spirit; for the Spirit searches all things, even the depths of God. For who among men knows the thoughts of a man except the spirit of the man which is in him? Even so the thoughts of God no one knows except the Spirit of God (1 Corinthians 2:10-11).

Therefore ask God to reveal His truth to you as He leads and guides you into all truth. He will if you will ask.

6. Each day when you finish your lesson, meditate on what you saw. Ask your heavenly Father how you should live in light of the truths you have just studied. At times, depending on how God has spoken to you through His Word, you might even want to write LFL ("Lessons for Life") in the margin of your Bible and then, as briefly as possible, record the lesson for life that you want to remember.

THIRD

This study is set up so that you have an assignment for every day of the week—so that you are in the Word daily. If you work through your study in this way, you will benefit more than if you do a week's study in one sitting. Pacing yourself this way allows time for thinking through what you learn on a daily basis!

The seventh day of each week differs from the other six days. The seventh day is designed to aid group discussion; however, it's also profitable if you are studying this book individually.

The "seventh" day is whatever day in the week you choose to finish your week's study. On this day, you will find a verse or two for you to memorize and STORE IN YOUR HEART. Then there is a passage to READ AND DISCUSS. This will help you focus on a major truth or major truths covered in your study that week.

We have included QUESTIONS FOR DISCUSSION OR INDIVIDUAL STUDY to assist those using this book in a Sunday school class or a group Bible study. Taking the time to answer these questions will help you apply the truth to your own life even if you are not doing this study with anyone else.

If you are in a group, be sure every member of the class, including the teacher, supports his or her answers and insights from the Bible text itself. Then you will be handling the Word of God accurately. As you learn to see what the text says and compare Scripture with Scripture, the Bible explains itself.

Always examine your insights by carefully observing the text to see what it *says.* Then, before you decide what the passage of Scripture *means,* make sure that you interpret it in the light of its context. Scripture will never contradict Scripture. If it ever seems to contradict the rest of the Word of God, you can be certain that something is being taken out of context. If you come to a passage that is difficult to understand, reserve your interpretations for a time when you can study the passage in greater depth.

The purpose of the Thought for the Week is to share with you what we consider to be an important element in your week of study. We have included it for your evaluation and, we hope, for your edification. This section will help you see how to walk in light of what you learned.

Books in the New Inductive Study Series are survey courses. If you want to do a more in-depth study of a particular book of the Bible, we suggest you do a Precept Upon Precept Bible study course on that book. You may obtain more information on these courses by contacting Precept Ministries International at 800-763-8280 or visiting our website at www.precept.org.

ROMANS

FINALLY FREE

Does living your life for God bring you joy and freedom? Or instead, does it leave you feeling guilty, as if you'll never be good enough to please God regardless of what you do? Do you hope that if you do enough good works, God will somehow overlook all your shortcomings and love you anyway?

Has the word *faith* lost its meaning for you? Has it become another overused Christian term that no longer has connection to your daily life? Does faith sometimes just feel like an empty wish?

If you feel like answering yes to some of these questions, you are not alone. Many Christians struggle with the power of sin and wonder if they can ever overcome it. But God has provided a solution to this problem! He gives us a reason to hope, as you will see for yourself in God's Word. Over the next several weeks as you study the book of Romans, you'll experience a deeper appreciation for what God has done for you, and you'll find freedom as you trust in His grace and love. This freedom is for real—it has been changing people's lives for centuries upon centuries.

Martin Luther struggled with these same issues while living as a monk nearly 500 years ago. He was tormented by guilt, so he fasted and prayed and put himself through all kinds of suffering, hoping that he could somehow tame his flesh and bring his sins under control. But nothing seemed to work for him. Trying to please God was a never-ending struggle, and he rarely found any victory despite all his efforts. He was left feeling a deep anguish in his soul.

But as he studied the book of Romans, just as you are doing today, he came to understand that righteousness comes only through faith, by trusting in God's grace to free us from the power of sin. Luther had been seeking righteousness in all the wrong ways. This insight changed him from a tortured soul in bondage to sin into a man who knew the deep and wondrous peace that only God can give.

What happened next? God used Luther to bring about the historic Protestant Reformation. The church was stuck in her idolatrous ways of trying to achieve righteousness through her own man-made rules. How was Luther transformed? The Holy Spirit used the very first chapter of this wonderful book of Romans! Then the Holy Spirit used Luther to transform the church! The church experienced an awesome revival as she returned to the liberating truths of Romans 1.

The book of Romans transformed Martin Luther, and it can transform you too. If you have struggled with pleasing God, trying every spiritual exercise people have commended to you for conforming yourself to God's holy Law, drop them all and start studying Romans immediately! If you are struggling to be *good enough* to please God, the message of Romans will set you free. It will assure you that faith in Christ alone, faith in His gospel, is all you need to be righteous in God's eyes. With this righteousness you have eternal life and peace with God now, and you will continue to live by faith.

But it doesn't stop with just feeling free. Romans will also show you that your day-to-day walk before God is a matter of faith—a faith that not only saves but also sanctifies (sets you apart and makes you different). Followers of Christ live each moment by faith. Faith will always be an indispensable part of your Christian walk for at least three reasons: (1) You will never be perfectly obedient, (2) day-to-day living can seem like a never-ending struggle to be good in God's eyes, and (3) we cannot please God without faith.

Romans will teach you about the all-powerful sovereign God, who always acts with infinite love, wisdom, justice, mercy, and faithfulness, and who, unlike man, does not change His mind after making promises. We need faith to accept the sovereignty of God over our lives, especially when circumstances get tough. We're never successful independent of God. Jesus said, "Apart from Me you can do nothing" (John 15:5).

Romans will even teach you how to serve God by living a life of faith under human government (even an evil government like first-century Rome), within a community of faith, and with all mankind. The righteous live by faith in every one of these environments.

Unlike any other letter in the New Testament, Romans explains basic truths and doctrines instead of addressing specific problems in the church. But that doesn't mean it isn't practical. It teaches fundamental truths we can base our lives on.

What a great treasure awaits you as you mine the precious jewels that lie in the book of Romans! Search diligently, dig deeply, and enjoy the fruit of your labor. The fruit is sweet and well worth the effort.

The Power of God for Salvation to Everyone Who Believes

∽∾∽∾

We often think of the gospel (the good news) as an important truth we should believe. But it is not only true; it is also powerful! It can change lives—our own as well as those of all who believe. If we have a heart for others that they might also experience the life-changing power of real faith, we need to know the gospel so we can share it.

At the outset of this book, Paul tells the Romans that he is not ashamed of the gospel because "it is the power of God for salvation to everyone who believes, to the Jew first and also to the Greek" (Romans 1:16). Paul knows it has the power to change everyone, and his passion is that all people would believe in this gospel and be saved.

In the first five chapters of Romans, Paul carefully lays out *why* both Greeks and Jews need salvation, and *how* salvation comes about. We could use many theological terms to communicate these truths, but we will focus on Romans' teachings about sin and death, faith and salvation, righteousness and unrighteousness.

When we have completed these first five weeks, perhaps we will understand how Martin Luther felt when his new faith set him free. Perhaps this will be a brand-new experience for you. It will definitely help you explain to others from Scripture how faith produces righteousness.

But knowing *how* to explain the gospel isn't enough, is it? We must be able to see our role in God's plan of salvation for the lost. The Almighty God of heaven and earth has written you, Beloved, into His enormous plan. He has given you His words of promise of rescue from the kingdom of darkness. In His wonderful gospel lies the path to the kingdom of everlasting light. Are you eager to be an important part of His plan for the world? Do you hunger to share the gospel? Do you really believe all people need salvation?

DAY ONE

Digging into the doctrines of Romans will be easier if we understand the historical setting of Paul's letter and his audience. In fact, when studying any letter, an important first step is to discover the historical setting by observing what you can about the author and recipients of the letter. Read Romans 1:1-15. Color code every reference to Paul (including pronouns) in one color, such as blue. Then list in a notebook what you learn about Paul.

Now read verses 1-15 again. This time, color code every reference to the recipients of this letter. Use orange or some other color of your choice. Then list what you learn about the recipients.

Now turn to Romans 15:15-32 and again color code the references to Paul and to the recipients. Add what you learn about each to the lists you made from Romans 1:1-15. Discovering the historical setting includes noting *where* things are taking place. Mark geographical references by double underlining them in green. Then think about *when* in Paul's ministry he is writing this letter. For some help, read the account in Acts 28:11-31 of his visit to Rome and compare it to what you saw in Romans 1:13.

Apart from these few verses, however, you will see the focus in Romans is not on Paul or those in Rome to whom he is writing. Rather, we will see that the focus is on the many foundational truths revealed in this book. All of the great doctrines of salvation are here. Like no other book, Romans lays out the path of salvation and the life of righteousness for every person. Once you capture the foundational truths in this book, you will be prepared to mine precious gems of truth throughout the entire Bible. Romans is a primary letter in that it helps set the stage for the wonderful message of the gospel of Jesus Christ. We often describe Romans as "The Constitution of Our Faith."

We will mark many key words throughout the 16 chapters of Romans. Some will be found in only a few chapters; others occur throughout the book. You'll need to make a bookmark with these key words on it. A three-by-five card works well for this. Make notes on your bookmark that remind you which words to mark in each chapter. If you are diligent in this, you will be rewarded with wonderful insights into the great teachings of sin, salvation, justification, and sanctification.

But this is not just a book of doctrines. You will also understand how to practically live your life in light of all the amazing things God has done for you. We have so much to observe, so much to learn. Are you ready?

DAY TWO

Some wise person once said, "Repetition is the mother of learning." In inductive Bible study, reading and rereading is a key to grasping the message. Today, read Romans 1:1-15 again and mark every reference to *Jesus* like this: **Jesus**. Use purple to draw the symbol and yellow to shade in the middle. When you're done, you may want to list what you learn about Jesus in a notebook that could contain all your notes from your study of Romans.

DAY *T*HREE

Read all of Romans 1 today and mark every reference to the *gospel* (including pronouns and synonyms) like this: **gospel**. Use red to make the megaphone and color it green. Also mark the words *faith* like this: **faith**, using purple to make the book and coloring it green. Mark *believe* the same way because they are the same Greek word—*faith* is the noun form, and *believe* is the verb form. Mark *grace* blue with a yellow border, and mark *wrath*[1] with a red *W*.

Marking the key words is important for a couple of reasons. It slows you down in your study and also makes words stand out on the page. Once you've marked the key words in your Bible, you are ready to make observations about them. Ask the 5 W's and an H about each key word—*who, what, when, where, why,* and *how*. Make a list for each word, noting what you learn from each reference. If marking words feels foreign to you, don't worry. We promise you that it is not busywork, nor is it just coloring your Bible. After you experiment with marking key words, you will see the value. It has an incredible effect on your observation of the text!

DAY *F*OUR

Read through Romans 1 again and mark *(un)righteous(ness)*.

This word does not appear many times in this chapter, but it is central to the message of this book. Either choose a color or mark *righteousness* with a big *R* and *unrighteousness* with a big *R* with a slash through it like this: **unrigh̸teousness**.

You may be tempted to simply mark the key words and move on in your study, but don't do it! Each time you mark a key word, take time to see what you can learn about it.

Notice Paul's mention of Jews and Gentiles. You don't need to mark these words, but they are important to observe. Watch out for synonyms for *Gentile* too. Sometimes Paul uses *Greek(s)* for *Gentile(s)*.

DAY FIVE

Romans 1 has a turning point at verse 18. Paul declares in verse 15 that he is eager to preach the gospel to those in Rome, and in verses 16-18 he gives three reasons, each starting with *for*. List Paul's three reasons in your notebook.

Romans 1:20-32 describes people who suppress the truth in unrighteousness. These verses include some key phrases to mark or underline: *exchanged*[2] and *God gave them over*.[3] Read Romans 1:20-32 and mark these phrases. Note the progression of events as you observe what the people did and how God responded. Write out what people exchanged like this: "They exchanged _____ for _____." Under each exchange, record how God responded with the phrase, "God gave them over _____." What is the culmination of this series of exchanges? In others words, where does it all lead to?

DAY SIX

Read through Romans 1 one more time. Now, let's reason

together. Think through this first chapter. Paul begins by identifying himself and his audience. He's an apostle to the Gentiles and is writing to the "beloved of God in Rome." From this first chapter, can you tell whether these "beloved" are Jews or Gentiles? Although Paul declares the gospel is for Jews *and* Gentiles in verse 16, what audience does he seem to be addressing in Romans 1? In Romans 1:20-32, as he depicts the regression of those who suppress the truth, whom is he describing? What is his main point about these people? Should they be excused because they had no idea God exists, or is God's wrath just? What verses show this? It is so important that you let the text answer these questions, even if you have to reexamine what you have believed over the years.

Read Psalm 19:1-3; 50:6; 97:6 and compare them to Romans 1:18-20.

When we study letters in the Bible, we can keep track of the progression of events and flow of thought by summarizing the main ideas of a chapter into a theme. Now that you have read chapter 1 several times this week, what would you say is the main theme of Romans 1? Record this on ROMANS AT A GLANCE on page 121.

DAY SEVEN

 Store in your heart: Romans 1:16-17
Read and discuss: Romans 1:16-32

QUESTIONS FOR DISCUSSION OR INDIVIDUAL STUDY

∾ What do you learn about those who suppress the truth in unrighteousness? What will be their fate?

∾ Do these people know about God? How? Are they without excuse? Show how the text supports your answer.

∾ Discuss what these people did. What did they exchange? How did God respond in each case? What did He give them over to?

∾ Based on what you learned in these verses, why do you think Paul wanted to preach the gospel to the Gentiles?

∾ What would Gentiles be saved from? How can they be saved?

∾ What has the power to save people who believe? What is the fate of those who do not believe? Do you think that power is still available, or was it limited to Paul's preaching? Have you ever seen that power at work?

∾ What questions come to mind that are not answered in this chapter? Remember, we have 12 more weeks of study in Romans to answer our questions. For now, simply write the questions down so you don't forget them as you study the book of Romans.

THOUGHT FOR THE WEEK

Paul wanted to preach the gospel to the Gentiles because it is the power of God for salvation to everyone who believes. In the gospel, the righteousness of God is revealed. But the wrath of God is also "revealed from heaven against all ungodliness and unrighteousness of men who suppress the truth in unrighteousness."

Everyone knows God exists because the creation itself shows His invisible attributes of eternal power and deity, His divine nature. Though these attributes are invisible, Paul says they are "clearly seen, being understood" through creation. God has shown all men His power and deity, so no man is excused before God. God's wrath on unrighteousness is just.

Even though all men knew God, they did not honor Him as God or give Him thanks. Professing to be wise, they became fools. The folly of man! The creation itself declares who God is and what His character is, but men devise other gods, other creatures, other products of their minds that are not God at all. Psalm 14:1 uses plain language to show that this endeavor is ridiculous: "The fool has said in his heart, 'There is no God.'"

All mankind had their chance to acknowledge God because God revealed Himself through the created world. A small group of people—the Jews—were eventually given the first Scriptures, the Old Testament. But from the very beginning, all mankind was given the creation. When mankind rejected God's revelation of Himself in creation, God gave them over to impurity, to degrading passions, and to a depraved mind. He gave them over to what they wanted. This resulted in a horrible set of exchanges.

This regression—a downward spiral into the ugly depths of depravity—included worshipping idols and other created things and committing acts of sexual depravity. It went from hearts to bodies, from minds to behavior. As a result, people received their due penalty. God is just. He gives people a chance to acknowledge Him, and when they refuse, He gives them their just reward—wrath.

Yet people continue to sneer at God and deny His existence. They deny that He created the world in the beginning and will judge it at the end. Even though they concede that such behavior is worthy of death (verse 32), they irrationally give hearty approval to others who continue in sin like themselves.

Misery loves company. Do you know anyone like this? Do

you have friends, neighbors, coworkers, or even family members who live a life that worships self, pleasure, and whatever makes them happy or feel good? We all do. Does your heart cry out to help them? Do you see their inevitable fate—the wrath of God—and do you want them to be saved from it?

This is our world—the world we live in, a world that is depraved and headed for judgment. But the gospel is the power of God for salvation to everyone who believes. This is good news!

The reality is this: Without Christ, people go to hell. The opportunity is this: With Christ, people can be saved. They can be rescued through the gospel—the saving message of the good news in Jesus Christ.

Do you believe in the gospel? Are you ready to deliver the good news to the lost?

THE JEWS ARE
WITHOUT EXCUSE

Have you noticed that whenever we make a mistake, our tendency is to find an excuse? Instead of admitting we were wrong, we try to think up good reasons why we didn't do what we were supposed to do. And we're really no different when we are dealing with God. But Romans reminds us that we have no excuse!

So here is something to think about: If Gentiles are without excuse because God showed Himself in creation, what about Jews? Were they excused because they had the Old Testament Law, which contained in great detail what God expected of His people? The Jews were confident that keeping the Law would make them righteous before God and help them escape His wrath against unrighteousness. And since they had the Law and knew what God wanted them to do, surely they were even more righteous (or so they thought) because they pointed out how far the Gentiles were from God. Weren't they showing God that they knew right from wrong? Wouldn't God consider them righteous because they had demonstrated His view of sin?

People who trust solely in their works—doing good deeds, joining a church, being good people, or things like these— are often the most difficult to reach with the gospel. They are religious, so they assume they must be pleasing to God. They may be humble, or they may wear their righteousness like a merit badge on their sleeves. Either way, their hearts are dark with sin and a pseudo righteousness. But self-appointed badges of good deeds don't fly with God. This is what many Jews of Paul's day were like. God doesn't justify anyone in this manner, as Paul shows in Romans 2.

DAY ONE

The Bible is God's idea. It is His means of revealing Himself to us. Therefore we get to know God by reading His Word, His revelation. Read Romans 2 today, and mark the reference to *Jesus* as you did last week. Mark each mention of *God* like this: **God** and the reference to the *Holy Spirit* like this: **Holy Spirit**. You will find just one reference to *Jesus* and one to the *Holy Spirit*, so don't miss them. Then add to your list from chapter 1 all that you learn in chapter 2 about Jesus, and begin similar lists for God and the Holy Spirit.

DAY TWO

We're going to add some more key words to our bookmark today that weren't in Romans 1. In Romans 2, we want to mark *Law* when it refers to the Law of Moses. In the New American Standard Bible, it is capitalized to distinguish it from man's laws. Mark it like this: **Law**. Also mark *judge (judgment)*.[4] Consider marking these words with a judge's gavel, like this: **judge**.

Color *sinned* brown. Now read Romans 2 again, marking these three new key words. As you have done before, continue listing what you learn about these key words. When you make your lists, remember to ask the 5 W's and an H. For example, look at each place you marked *judge* and ask questions like these: Who judges? What is judged? Who is judged? How or by what are things judged?

DAY THREE

Read through Romans 2 again today, marking *unrighteousness* as well as *wrath*. Use the marking system you recorded in your bookmark last week. Also mark the words *Jew* and *Gentile*. Then list in your notebook what you learn from marking these key words. Remember that when you make your lists, write down what the text says, letting it speak for itself. If your notes start with "What it means to me is…" you have ventured into interpretation and are skipping the foundational step of observing the text. At this stage of your study you simply want to record the facts as found in the text.

DAY FOUR

Read through this rich chapter one more time! We're going to study three new key words: *justify (justified, justifier), circumcision,* and *uncircumcision (uncircumcised).* Mark *circumcision* with a red knife like this: **circumcision** and mark *uncircumcision* in the same way but put a slash through it like this: **uncircumcision**.

And again, list what you learned as you marked. Think through the relationships between righteousness, circumcision, judgment, and the Law. Take your time. Understanding these truths is vital to understanding our own salvation.

DAY FIVE

Circumcision was a one-time act performed on male Hebrews. God gave Abraham this sign as a reminder of His promise that Abraham's descendants would be a people for His name. Read Genesis 17:7-14 to see how it began. According to God's command to the Israelites in the Old Testament, the practice of circumcision was the cutting off the foreskin of the baby boy. This action signified that he was in a right relationship to God through the covenant. By the first century AD, the Jews had become so identified with the rite that they were frequently called "the circumcision." See Galatians 2:12; Ephesians 2:11; Colossians 4:11; Titus 1:10 for examples.

In Romans 2, you will see that Paul expands the concept of circumcision beyond the mere taking away of flesh. He also does this in Philippians 3:2-3 and Colossians 2:11.

What kind of circumcision does God actually want? Why did He command Abraham to circumcise his flesh? We'll see the answer in Romans 4.

DAY SIX

Think about Paul's mention of the Law and circumcision. These weren't mentioned in Romans 1. Why not? Is Paul now addressing a different group of people? If so, whom? Jew or Gentile? If you're uncertain, read Romans 2:17-27 again.

Read Romans 2:28-29. How does Paul define *Jew*? What does he mean? Has Israel missed the point of God's covenant with Abraham? Look at the contrasts made in verse 29. What do you learn about the Jews' understanding of their circumcision?

Review the references to the Law in Romans 2. Are people

justified simply by having the Law or having the sign of the covenant? What verses help you answer this?

Summarize the main point or idea of Romans 2 and record it on ROMANS AT A GLANCE on page 121.

DAY SEVEN

 Store in your heart: Romans 2:11

Read and discuss: Romans 2

QUESTIONS FOR DISCUSSION OR INDIVIDUAL STUDY

- ❧ Describe Paul's use of the word *judgment* in Romans 2:1-16. Who is judged? Who judges? By what standard are we judged? Why are people judged? What comes as a result of judgment?

- ❧ What is the relationship between the Law and being just?

- ❧ What does Paul accuse Jews of thinking about themselves?

- ❧ Does pointing out someone else's sin make you more righteous than he is? Does it make you feel more righteous? Why do we sometimes do this?

- ❧ What does Paul ask those who bear the name *Jew* to consider in 2:17-24? What questions does he ask?

- ❧ According to what you read in Genesis, what did circumcision indicate? How did the Jew of Paul's time view circumcision? What is "true circumcision"?

- ❧ Is the most important circumcision outward or inward? What is the difference?

∾ What outward signs of being a Christian do you have? Does being baptized or joining a local church save you and make you a Christian? Are you a Christian because you were born to Christian parents?

∾ What is your relationship to the Law? Are you a hearer or a doer? Does mere adherence to rules prove you are just? How much do the inward motivations matter? Why?

∾ What do you think will be the outcome for yourself "on that day when…God will judge the secrets of men through Christ Jesus" (verse 16)?

THOUGHT FOR THE WEEK

We can make many mistakes in life. One of them is trusting in something or someone who is unable to help us. We can trust in our own physical strength up to a point, but something is always too strong for us. We can trust in our knowledge, but we will always bump into something we do not know. We can trust in our heritage, our lineage, our birthright, but someone could demean this status. So what is left to trust in?

So it is with our relationship to God. Knowing the Law doesn't help the Jew escape judgment. Being born a Jew doesn't clear the guilt, and being circumcised doesn't help. Like physical circumcision, being baptized and joining a Christian church are not enough; they are only outward signs. What matters is not just the outward appearances, but what is inside. The critical issue is whether *works* or *faith alone* will save us from judgment. Which one will it be?

God is not partial. He is "no respecter of persons" (Acts 10:34 KJV). The point is that who you are, your possessions, your knowledge, and your abilities can't help you when God judges. God's righteous judgment depends on what you actually do, not what you talk about or claim to do. God is also very concerned with the motivation behind your good works.

We learned this week that if you do the very thing you tell other people they should not do, you will be judged as they are. You will be motivated by hollow superiority, as was the Jew that Paul addressed in Romans 2. It's simply hypocrisy—judging others for things you do yourself.

The Jews Paul is referring to in chapter 2 judged the Gentiles because the Jews were God's chosen people; they had the special revelation of God in the Law, and no other nation was related to God as His people. They were therefore righteous in their *own* eyes, and they declared the Gentiles unrighteous, pointing out their sins and condemning them. They missed the point that God gave them the laws and covenants so they would be a light to the nations. Instead of fulfilling their calling, they turned the light in on themselves, leaving the world in darkness.

What about us? Do Christians do the same thing? Do we feel superior, as if our identification as Christians makes us better than others? What is our motivation? Do we feel one up when we know the Bible better than someone else? Do we believe we're closer to God because of our knowledge or strength or church membership?

What brings praise from God? Do we think lightly of the riches of His kindness and tolerance and patience, or do we bow humbly before Him in gratitude? When we identify wrong beliefs and attitudes toward God, toward sin, toward righteousness—in ourselves or in others—what do we do?

Look inward and ask yourself what you trust in. Take some time to reflect on this question: Are you like the Jews who trust in the Law? What will you do? Ask the Spirit to search your heart and reveal to you any patterns of hypocrisy or attitudes of self-righteousness. As He reveals those to you, confess them to Him as sin and ask Him to forgive you.

Do you know anyone who fits this description? Ask God to show you where you stand before you turn to others. If you stand in the confidence of His grace, bow humbly before Him in gratitude and ask Him to show you how to reach those around you who do not know the riches of His kingdom. Pray, Beloved. Lives hang in the balance!

Both Jews and Gentiles Need Salvation

In Romans 1, Paul established that the Gentiles are sinners in need of salvation. Starting in Romans 2 and continuing in Romans 3, Paul shows that the Jews are sinners in need of salvation too. In Romans 2 we saw that their circumcision of the flesh or possession of the Law does not make them righteous. Did being a Jew or being circumcised have any advantage at all? The answer is in Romans 3.

Beloved, this will be a week that could change your life. As you read Romans 3, you will discover some terms that are basic to the gospel: *justification*, *redemption*, and *propitiation*. Christians use these terms, but how many could use the Scriptures to explain exactly what each of these and other basic doctrines mean?

The truths you will be studying are the very bedrock on which your salvation rests! It is so important that you, a child of God, understand the precious truths contained in these doctrines. We live in an age when people are tossed to and fro and carried about by every wind of doctrine (Ephesians 4:14). You are responsible to know and to speak of things that are fitting for sound doctrine (Titus 2:1).

DAY ONE

Read Romans 3:1-8 in the light of Romans 2. Paul didn't write his letter with chapter divisions, and he continues the thought from Romans 2 right through to Romans 3:8. See if you can discern how it fits together. Also, note Paul's style in Romans of asking a question he supposes someone else has asked and then answering it himself. Such is the opening sentence of Romans 3.

Now Read Romans 3:1-8 again and mark any key words or phrases from your bookmark.

DAY TWO

Read through Romans 3:1-8 again, marking the phrase *May it never be!*[5] This phrase is a translation of an emphatic *No!* in New Testament Greek. You'll see this phrase several times in Romans, so add it to your bookmark.

Now, list the questions Paul asks in Romans 3:1-8. Beside each one, list his answer.

What is the conclusion we should reach about God's judgment from these verses? On whom does it belong? Is it just? How can you back up your answers?

DAY THREE

Read Romans 3:8-20, marking key words and phrases from your bookmark. Watch the pronouns *we* and *they* in Romans 3:9 and mark them accordingly. Paul makes a couple of really powerful and important statements in these verses that you will want to underline or highlight in some way.

Note what you learn about God and the Law.

DAY FOUR

In Romans 1:18–3:20, Paul dealt with one basic issue—sin. Quickly read over this segment, and look at the repetition of the word *sin*. Romans 1:18-32 shows that Gentiles are sinners, that even though they had revelation from God in creation, they chose their own way. Romans 2:1–3:8 shows that Jews also are sinners even though they had revelation from God in circumcision and the Law.

With respect to these facts, what general conclusion does Paul draw in Romans 3:9-18? (See especially Romans 3:9-10.)

Beginning in Romans 3:19-20, Paul turns to the Law. Does obeying the Law justify anyone in God's sight? Write this down; understanding this point is absolutely crucial.

If the Law does not justify man, what does the Law do? Write this down as well.

DAY FIVE

Today, read Romans 3:21-31 and mark the key words and phrases from your bookmark.

Paul has clearly demonstrated that Jews and Gentiles are sinners—that no one is righteous. Now he turns to the subject of *how* one is justified. Don't miss the clear statement of *how* God's righteousness is manifested. Mark it, highlight it, underline it, but most of all, take it into your heart and be confident in it.

DAY SIX

Now read Romans 3:21-31 again. Focus in on Romans 3:29-31 and the relationship between the Law, circumcision, Jews, and Gentiles. What is Paul saying?

Meditate on these truths today. See if you can outline the points in Paul's reasoning in Romans 1:18–3:31 about sin and righteousness. It may help to simply read through each phrase separately and then ask and answer the 5 W's and an H. Take your time doing this exercise. Writing it out on a sheet of paper will help you unpack these great truths.

Don't forget to record the theme of Romans 3 on ROMANS AT A GLANCE.

DAY SEVEN

 Store in your heart: Romans 3:10,23,28
Read and discuss: Romans 3:21-31

QUESTIONS FOR DISCUSSION OR INDIVIDUAL STUDY

- ∾ Briefly review and discuss what Paul demonstrated in Romans 1:18-32.

- ∾ Review and discuss what Paul proves in Romans 2:1–3:20.

- ∾ Together, what does this say? How does Paul summarize this in chapter 3? What verses would you use to summarize?

- ∾ Using the text, answer this question: How do circumcision and the Law relate to righteousness?

∾ Who is a sinner? Who is righteous? Who needs justification?

∾ How is anyone justified? List the points.

∾ Perhaps you would like to recite your memory verses from the last three weeks to solidify your understanding: Romans 1:16-17; 2:11; 3:10,23,28. You need to repeat them regularly. We suggest writing them on note cards and carrying them with you—in the car, at work, and home. Then you can live by them.

Thought for the Week

The grand conclusion of Paul's argument about sin is that no one is righteous—no Jew, no Gentile, no one. On his own, no one really understands; no one truly seeks God. Paul quotes Psalms and Isaiah to prove that God has declared these things true—even to the Jew who thinks he is righteous before God because he is circumcised and has the Law.

The Jew is deceived when he thinks that he can perfectly keep the law. He is deceived in his thinking he is keeping the Law and is thus made righteous. God revealed in His Word that this is not so. The Jew likes to tell the Gentile how righteous Jews are because they have the Law and because no one can ever be righteous without it. God pops his balloon with the truth that the Law defines sin and makes men conscious of it; it doesn't take sin away. We are all in the same sinking ship.

God is righteous. Man is unrighteous. How then can the two be reconciled? Paul answers, articulating clearly:

∾ The righteousness of God is available through faith in Jesus Christ. Faith alone—not works, not the Law—in Christ alone.

- ∾ The righteousness of God is available to all who believe, whether Jews or Gentiles. God is not partial.

- ∾ Justification is a gift of God's grace. Man cannot earn it or purchase it and definitely does not deserve it.

- ∾ Justification is secured only through redemption in Christ Jesus. We are redeemed, which literally means we are purchased out of bondage. An exchange occurs. Christ Jesus paid the price for our freedom.

- ∾ God publicly displayed Jesus as a propitiation (a sin offering) through faith in His blood, passing over sins previously committed.

The crux of the matter is Christ's propitiation and our faith in His blood. What is propitiation? *Propitiation* comes from the Greek word *hilasterion*, which refers to God's passing over sin (as He did in the Passover in Exodus 12 when He saw the blood covering the doorway).

Propitiation carries the idea of satisfaction. It is more than mere payment or expiation, which meets the heavy obligations of justice; it advances to the satisfaction of the one to whom a debt is owed. The only payment that satisfies justice is sinless blood. Here is the problem—we do not have sinless blood, so we cannot pay our debt. Jesus does, and He pays our debt for us. God is fully satisfied with Christ's sacrifice. He harbors no ill will toward us, those who injured Him. Instead, He loves us.

The most striking aspect of this payment is that we cannot pay it. We do not have the means to offer sinless blood because we are sinners, not sinless. We cannot earn or purchase the payment ourselves. Christ substituted Himself for us in the payment of our debt to God. He paid our just debt, and God is satisfied, or pleased (see Isaiah 53:10).

This is true for both Jew and Gentile. Because all have

sinned and fallen short of the glory of God, none is righteous, not even one. Jews and Gentiles share the same path to righteousness—we are all on the same plan for salvation.

That same path requires only one thing: faith. Faith alone in the payment Christ made when He died on the cross, shedding His sinless blood. *Faith alone* simply means trust, believing that Jesus has paid the price. This justification is a gift of grace—God's favor to us, which we simply do not deserve.

Remember, Beloved, truth is revealed precept upon precept. Precepts are like building blocks. Learning is a building process, so do not become discouraged. Do not look at the architect's plans and think, *It's too much for me.* Take it step by step, principle by principle, brick by brick. When you have finished, stand back in awe and admire what has been built. You will be so thankful that you pressed on instead of giving up in dismay. The plodders eventually accomplish things—not the wishers, the dreamers, or the talkers, but the consistent doers.

The Promise
of Abraham

Paul has just completed his explanation in Romans 3 that man is justified by faith apart from works of the Law, that God justifies both circumcised Jews and uncircumcised Gentiles through faith. Jews and Gentiles are justified in the same manner—through faith in the reconciling sacrifice, the sinless blood of Christ. At the end of Romans 2, Paul asserts that God does not desire mere outward conformance to the letter of the Law, but rather, inward renewal according to the spirit of the Law.

In Romans 4, Paul will continue to make his case of justification by faith alone. The first witness he calls to the stand will be the famous Father Abraham. Paul will use Abraham to illustrate the role of circumcision, the Law, and faith in the life of the believer. Abraham was the first person God commanded to be circumcised. But (and this is the key point) he believed God, and this faith was credited to him as righteousness *before* he was circumcised. You will also be reminded that Abraham came before Moses and the giving of the Law.

As you study, remember that these truths apply to us too! Whether they are new to you or old hat, meditate on them.

Drink in the truth that what was true for Abraham is true for us: Our faith is what pleases God.

DAY ONE

Read Romans 4:1-12, marking the key words and noting the things you have listed on your bookmark. The list of what you should mark is getting long, so we're going to break the chapter up into segments to help you. Don't get bogged down and miss the message—it's exciting!

DAY TWO

Read Romans 4:1-12 again and mark *credited*.[6] This English word is used only in this chapter, so you don't need to add it to your bookmark for Romans. List what you learn from marking *credited*. Ask the 5 W's and an H. What is credited? To whom? On what basis? When is it credited?

The English words *credited*, *reckoned*, and *accounted* are translations of the Greek word *logizomai*, an accounting term meaning to "reckon, account, predicate, credit to one's account." In this context, a credit is something added to your account, something someone else has given you. It is the opposite of a debit, which in this sense would be something you give up or lose to someone.

List what you learn from marking *circumcision*. Why was circumcision given? Summarize in a few words the relationship between faith, circumcision, and righteousness.

DAY THREE

Now read Romans 4:13-25, marking the key words and phrases on your bookmark. You won't find *circumcision* in these verses, but you will find *credited*. Mark the word *promise* and note how it relates to Abraham.

DAY FOUR

God's promise to Abraham is one of the most important in all of Scripture. Read Genesis 12:1-3 and make a list of everything that God promises Abraham.

What was God's plan to "bless all the families of the earth" through Abraham? Read Genesis 15:1-7 to answer this question. If you see anything else that God promised to Abraham, add it to the list you started above.

In Galatians 3, Paul addresses believers who seem to have forgotten that they received the Holy Spirit through faith, not through conformity to the Law. He then explains the way God's promise to Abraham relates to the Law, sin, faith, and justification—all subjects included in our study of Romans thus far.

So today, read Galatians 3:1-18 and mark the same key words you marked in Romans 4. In Galatians 3, you will see some other key words that you might want to mark, such as *blessing, curse,* and *covenant*. We'll be marking *covenant* a little later in Romans. You will see how these two powerful chapters dovetail theologically, and you will learn some additional information about the Law in Galatians that Paul did not include in Romans.

DAY FIVE

Today, read Galatians 3:19-29, marking as you did yesterday. Notice how Paul anticipates questions and then answers them as he did in Romans. What are the main questions he asks in Galatians 3? Also notice (and mark) the phrase *May it never be!* Read carefully to see how Paul answers his own questions.

DAY SIX

How do Romans 4 and Galatians 3 fit together? See if you can briefly outline the main points that Paul makes in these two chapters about Abraham, faith, justification, the promise, sin, and the Law. This will be very helpful in understanding these great truths.

Remember to add the theme of Romans 4 to ROMANS AT A GLANCE.

DAY SEVEN

 Store in your heart: Romans 4:3

Read and discuss: Romans 4; Galatians 3

QUESTIONS FOR DISCUSSION OR INDIVIDUAL STUDY

- ∾ How was Abraham declared righteous by God? Discuss what Romans 4 and Galatians 3 say about faith and righteousness.

- ∾ Discuss the relationship between Abraham's righteousness and circumcision. Which came first? Does anyone need to be circumcised to be righteous?

~ Discuss the relationship between Abraham's righteousness and the Law. Which came first?

~ Some people say that the way to be righteous in the Old Testament was different from the way to be righteous in the New Testament. How would you answer?

~ Some people say that when the Law came to Israel, keeping it was the way to be righteous before God. What would you answer from Romans 4 and Galatians 3? What relationship did the Law have to the promise (or covenant) God gave to Abraham? (Hint: see Galatians 3:19.) Did the Law cancel out the promise to Abraham?

~ What was the purpose of the Law? What was it supposed to do for man?

~ Galatians 3:8,16 adds a very important fact about Abraham's faith. What did Abraham believe?

~ Do Paul's teachings in Romans about Jews and Gentiles agree with what he teaches in Galatians?

~ How has this study of Romans 4 and Galatians 3 changed your view of justification or your opinion about the relationships between God's promise to Abraham, the Law, and your personal salvation?

Thought for the Week

In Genesis 22, Abraham obediently traveled with his promised son (whom he loved), Isaac, to the land of Moriah to offer a sacrifice to God. God had asked Abraham to sacrifice Isaac even though God had told him that Isaac would be the one through whom He would raise up a great nation.

When they reached the mountain God showed them,

Abraham took the wood, the knife, and the fire, and he told his servants to wait for him and Isaac. They planned to go worship God and then return. When Isaac asked where the sacrificial animal was, Abraham replied that God Himself would provide a lamb.

Hebrews 11:17-19 tells us that Abraham had faith in God's ability to raise Isaac from the dead and fulfill His promise of a great nation through Isaac's seed. This is one of the most glorious Old Testament types (foreshadowings) of God offering up His only begotten Son, the Lamb of God, as a sacrifice for the sins of man. Abraham had given up Isaac emotionally. Accordingly, the writer of Hebrews says that Abraham received Isaac back—as a type. This picture in some ways prefigures Christ's resurrection and ascension to the Father.

We saw in Galatians 3:8 that the gospel was preached beforehand to Abraham—the message that all the nations would be blessed in him. This gospel is called the promise in Galatians 3:16 with the added truth that the blessing would come through Jesus. Jesus told the Pharisees, "Abraham rejoiced to see My day, and he saw it and was glad" (John 8:56). God credited the righteousness of this new faith to Abraham's account. Abraham neither worked for it nor deserved it.

Romans 4 and Galatians 3 clearly show that Jews and Gentiles are declared righteous on the very same basis—by faith in the gospel of Jesus Christ. And we saw that God first credited righteousness to Abraham *before* circumcision and even *before* the Law. After the introduction of circumcision and the Law, God continued (and continues!) to credit this same righteousness to those who believe.

We also learn from these chapters that although the Law came 400 years after God's promise to Abraham, it did not nullify the promise or change the way men become righteous before God. Faith remained the only basis for righteousness. God added the Law because of transgression. The Law defined sin, becoming man's "tutor" (Galatians 3:24). The Greek word for *tutor* sounds like our word *pedagogue* and literally means "child-leader." The Law leads us to Christ because it proves unequivocally that no person can consistently keep it—no one can achieve through self-effort the sinless perfection required by the Law.

The Law requires two different things: First, it requires death to satisfy the (negative) penal debt of sin. Second, it demands righteousness to satisfy the (positive) requirement of perfection—thus, the death of a sinless, perfect person. It proves that we need to continue to believe the promise God made to Abraham and not revert to any system of law to become righteous before God. Only God can give us the perfect righteousness of Christ that the Law requires. He gives it by grace through faith—the same faith Abraham had in the everlasting gospel.

The Lord offers this righteousness not only to the Jews immediately descended from Abraham, Isaac, and Jacob, but to all mankind—Gentiles included. You and I and anyone else not physically descended from Abraham can become children of Abraham and heirs to the promise of grace through faith by believing the same thing Abraham believed—the gospel of Jesus Christ.

Only now we know His name. The prophets looked for His coming—the time of the Messiah's appearing. They knew the place was Bethlehem of Judah, and they knew the lineage was David's, but they didn't know when...until Jesus came. But most of His brethren of the circumcision and of the Law didn't believe and receive Him.

Jesus inaugurated the new covenant prophesied by Jeremiah and Ezekiel (Jeremiah 31:31-34; Ezekiel 36:26-27). This covenant, founded on the blood of the Son of God (Acts 20:28; 1 Corinthians 11:25), promised a new heart on which God's Law would be written and a new spirit that would cause the new heart to continue walking in God's statutes.

Everyone dies because all have sinned and fallen short of the glory of God. "There is none righteous, not even one." But God in His mercy has provided a way for you and me to escape His just sentence of everlasting death. God sent His Son, Jesus, who knew no sin, to die for us on the cross, to pay the price for sin that we owed. And He overcame death through His resurrection, which guarantees that those who believe in Him—in His death, burial, resurrection, and atonement for sin—will be saved from death and have eternal life.

Just like Abraham!

Does this thrill you? Can you rejoice in God's gracious plan to redeem you? Does your heart leap at the idea of enjoying life eternal, just like Abraham? If you have believed God as Abraham did, you have the same righteousness, the same salvation. Praise God for His gracious gift!

If you haven't believed, why not believe today? There's so much to gain!

THROUGH THE ONE MAN

Have you ever met anyone who doubted God's love? Possibly that person wondered, "How could God let His Son die for someone who was set against Him?" Or maybe you have heard this line: "Well, if God loves me so much, why am I having all this trouble?"

Maybe you have met others who have asked these questions, or maybe you have asked them yourself. What are the answers? They are found, Beloved, in Romans 5.

DAY ONE

Read Romans 5:1-11 and mark the key words and phrases from your bookmark.

The chapter starts with the word *therefore* (as does the section beginning in verse 12), so we know that whatever Paul says in these first 11 verses is based on what he just finished saying in chapter 4 or perhaps all of Romans 1–4. Since we have been dealing with the subject of justification in Romans 1–4, what purpose does *therefore* in Romans 5:1 serve?

DAY TWO

Read Romans 5:1-11 again, and in your notebook, list four truths about those who are justified (you may find more, but list at least four).

DAY THREE

Let's look more closely at the progression of thought in Romans 5:3-5. Three times in Romans 5:2-11, Paul says "we exult," giving us three things to exult in. Find these three occurrences of *exult* and list them in your notebook.

The Greek word translated *exult*[7] here is the same word translated *boast*[8] in Romans 2:17,23; 4:2. Contrast the boasting in these verses to what you see in chapter 5. Then think about why we might boast or exult in what Romans 5:3-5 says.

What does Romans 5:6-11 add for our exultation? What happened for us, and when did it happen? What did God demonstrate for us, and how did He do it? This is extremely important to grasp—what God did wasn't something we earned. We didn't first "clean up our act" so God would love us and Christ would die for us. He died for us while we were...

Romans 5:6—

Romans 5:8—

Romans 5:10—

Wow! Take a moment and give thanks to a God who reaches out to us with a love so undeserved!

DAY FOUR

Read Romans 5:12-21 and mark the key words and phrases

from your bookmark. Mark *gift* and *reign* in these verses and add them to your bookmark.

List what you learn about *gift*. What is the gift? Who received it? Who gave it? What brought about the gift?

DAY FIVE

The main argument of Romans 5:12-21 includes a contrast between what two characters?

Read through this text and mark the two characters separately. Also mark the word *through*, which you'll find six times in verses 18-21. It must be an important word if Paul repeated it so much!

List what Romans 5:12-14 says happened through the one man, Adam. How does the *gift* fit in?

Then list what is true of the One. Who is the One? What did He do? How does this contrast with Adam?

Remember Romans 5:12-16. You'll see a succinct restatement of it next week in Romans 6:23.

DAY SIX

Don't forget to add the theme of Romans 5 to ROMANS AT A GLANCE. If you've been filling out this chart faithfully, you'll notice that these chapters form a segment. What is the common subject of this segment? Record it in the space provided on ROMANS AT A GLANCE.

From ROMANS AT A GLANCE, you also ought to be able to see the flow of thought so far in Romans. See if the chapter themes you've recorded give you the main gist of Paul's discussion thus far. You can always change your themes as you review them.

You may even discern some subsegments within these five chapters. What subject is dealt with in Romans 1:18–3:20? Then what subject is in Romans 3:21–5:21? If you can see these segments, record the common topic in another column on ROMANS AT A GLANCE and draw a horizontal line to separate them at the appropriate place.

If you've got extra time, review Genesis 2:15–3:19. It will help you understand Paul's comments in Romans 5 about Adam, sin, and death.

DAY SEVEN

 Store in your heart: Romans 5:8
Read and discuss: Romans 5

QUESTIONS FOR DISCUSSION OR INDIVIDUAL STUDY

- ✺ What is the significance of Romans 5:1? Having peace with God implies what is over? How does Romans 1:18-32 relate to Romans 5:1?

- ✺ Discuss the ways righteousness, grace, gift, credit, and wages relate to each other.

- ✺ Discuss what we have as a result of being justified.

- ✺ Is boasting wrong? Should we boast in what God has done for us? Is that different from boasting in ourselves? What in Romans 5 helps you answer this?

- ✺ List and discuss the results of Adam's fall.

- ✺ From Romans 5:15-19, list and discuss blessings that have come to us through the One, Jesus.

∽ Review Romans 5:12-21. What contrasts do you see between justification and judgment?

∽ Paul uses the word *through* six times in Romans 5:18-21. What is Paul teaching by using this word?

∽ Summarize Paul's teaching in Romans 1:18–3:20.

∽ Summarize the flow of thought in Romans 3:21–5:21.

∽ How do Romans 1–5 fit together?

THOUGHT FOR THE WEEK

When God created the heavens and the earth, He created man in His image. He created a man and a woman and told them they could eat freely of the fruit of any tree in the garden except the tree of the knowledge of good and evil. He said that in the day that they ate of that fruit, they would surely die.

Eve took that fruit and ate and gave it to her husband, Adam. He ate as well. In that one act, sin entered the world, and death through sin. The tree of life was also in the garden. Had they eaten its fruit, they would have lived forever in the state of sin.

The first man and woman were sent into exile. God cast them out of the garden to toil in the world. He guarded the tree of life with cherubim. But He promised them a seed who would eventually defeat Satan, the serpent. He provided a cover for their nakedness by shedding the blood of an animal.

In Romans 5, Paul takes us back to the Garden of Eden, to the first man, Adam, and the first sin. In Romans 5 we learn that this one act introduced sin and death into the world. Because of this single act of one man, everyone would now encounter death.

Paul contrasts this with the single act of the Righteous One,

Jesus, who overturned what Adam did. He is the promised seed of Genesis 3:15, the One who defeats Satan. According to Hebrews 2:14-15, Jesus died so that "through death He might render powerless him who had the power of death, that is, the devil, and free those who through fear of death were subject to slavery all their lives."

God accomplished this great act of reconciliation as a gift to us. In grace, motivated by love, and while we were yet sinners, God sent His only begotten Son to die in our place that we might live.

> But God, being rich in mercy, because of His great love with which He loved us, [notice when this happened:] even when we were dead in our transgressions, made us alive together with Christ (by grace you have been saved), and raised us up with Him, and seated us with Him in the heavenly places in Christ Jesus, so that in the ages to come He might show the surpassing riches of His grace in kindness toward us in Christ Jesus (Ephesians 2:4-7).

Sin once reigned through death, but those who receive the abundance of grace and the gift of righteousness will now reign in life through Jesus Christ.

What do we have now that we are justified by faith? We have peace with God. The war is over; we are no longer enemies—we are reconciled.

And what do we have to look forward to? We can exult in the glory of God. We can also exult in tribulations because we know that tribulation brings about perseverance, and perseverance brings about proven character, and proven character brings about hope, and hope does not disappoint. We have the Holy Spirit. We have eternal life. We will reign. Thanks be to God for His indescribable gift!

SHALL WE SIN SO GRACE MAY INCREASE?

For five chapters, Paul has expounded on what God has done for us in salvation. He has carefully explained that all men, Jews and Gentiles, are sinners without excuse before God. None are righteous. He has clearly proven that men can be justified before God only by faith in the One—Jesus Christ—and not by the works of the Law.

Salvation brings us under the reign of grace, but where does that leave the Christian in respect to sin? I am saved by grace, but does that give me license to sin? Shall we who are dead to sin live any longer in it?

Paul answers with a resounding "May it never be!"

DAY ONE

Read Romans 6:1-15 and mark the key words and phrases from your bookmark. This chapter is usually identified as the start of a new segment—Paul's teaching on sanctification. The question he asks in Romans 6:1 and the answer he gives in Romans 6:2-14 are really, however, just a continuation of the explanation of justification he so eloquently laid out in Romans 1–5. Systematic theologies often describe the doctrines of justification and sanctification distinctly. But as you will see in Romans 6, they are bound together in a beautiful package!

As you read and mark these verses, don't get distracted and simply color the text. Think hard about how this passage relates to what you have seen in Romans 1–5. As you mark the text, make lists so you can understand the flow of thought.

DAY TWO

Did you see any other words that were repeated and important enough to mark? Today we're going to add some new key words to mark in Romans 6–8, so read Romans 6:1-14 again, this time marking references to *death (dead, died)*, *life (alive, lives)*, *master*,[9] *slaves*,[10] and *freed from sin*. Some of these are used only in Romans 6 and others in Romans 6–8, but adding them to your bookmark will help you.

Again, watch for the flow of thought and how it answers the question in Romans 6:1. Remember to keep chapter 6 in the context you have already observed in chapters 1–5. Take your time working through this chapter, asking the 5 W's and an H and comparing it to what you have learned so far. Make lists that help you see Paul's line of reasoning.

DAY THREE

Here are some key terms we must be careful to understand: *old self*[11] and *body of sin* in Romans 6:6 and *mortal body* or *members*[12] *of your body* in Romans 6:12-13. We need to define these terms in agreement with Romans 1–5 and the rest of the

New Testament. If we don't clearly understand these terms, we'll be confused by conflicting teachings on this subject. We need to be solidly grounded so that we can stand in the truth.

Read Romans 6:5-6 again and note what is true "if we have become united with Him" and what we should know. What or who was crucified with Christ? What was God's purpose? From the grammatical construction of the English text, is the crucifixion of our old self something that happened in the past or something we continually do? (The Greek aorist tense supports *was* better than the *is* in the KJV.) Write your answer as a statement in your notebook.

The old self was crucified so that our body of sin might be "done away with." This phrase, which the King James Version renders as "destroyed," is a translation of a Greek phrase that literally means "rendered powerless or useless, made inactive." Something was empowering sin and making us slaves to it. Is "the body of sin" our physical body or our old self? These are deep questions, diligent student, but we must think them through and understand, or we will be likely to live in confusion and defeat all our lives.

DAY FOUR

Read Romans 6:7. What is the result of the old self being crucified with Christ?

Now read Romans 6:11-13. In your notebook, list three things we are told to do.

The English word *consider*[13] is the same one used for God accounting or reckoning Abraham righteous on the basis of his faith. In this context, it speaks about how believers should think about themselves. Don't miss the progression from Romans 6:11 to verses 12-14.

"It's Greek to me!" Here's some good news: You don't have to master the language to appreciate the observations that come from studying the original words in Greek. Using simple tools, you will discover that the Greek verb tenses used here show that we should *continually* consider ourselves dead to sin. This is not a one-time thought but rather a mind-set, an ongoing way of living.

The commands in Romans 6:12-13 are prohibitions. Some of the Romans who professed faith were doing these things, and Paul says, "Stop!" Think it through: Paul has said your old self has been crucified so that your body of sin might be rendered powerless, and he gives you these three commands to follow in response.

Answer the following questions from the text:

1. Whatever was crucified is already dead. What was crucified? What do we do with what has already been crucified and is dead? What do we do with ourselves now?

2. Whatever is mortal can still die. What do we live in now? What do we do with what is still living?

It is so important that you discover truth for yourself. As we continue with Romans 6–8, you will understand more. We need to lay a firm foundation here, though, so we don't get confused in the next two chapters.

DAY FIVE

Read and mark Romans 6:15-23. Be sure to mark any other key repeated words you may find in the text. Notice that Paul anticipates another question here and answers it with our now familiar "May it never be!"

Also note that Romans 6:16 starts with "Do you not know?" just as Romans 6:3 does. Both questions in Romans 6 deal with sin and grace, and both are answered with things believers are expected to know. The first question was about our identification with Christ in his death. What is this question about, and what is the basis of the answer?

DAY SIX

In Romans 6:15-23, Paul once again deals with past and present. List what he says the Romans were—what they did in the past.

Now list what they are—what they do now. What does he tell them they *should* do now?

Notice that he is speaking about their "members." What are these "members"?

Romans 6:19 uses the word *flesh* for the first time in this chapter. In the context of other terms and phrases you see, such as *old man*, *yourselves*, *mortal body*, and *members*, what does *flesh* refer to in this context? The Greek word is different from the one used for *body*. How does *flesh* relate to the mortal body and its members, and how does it relate to your *self*? These are deep questions, Beloved. If your head hurts right now, don't worry. The answers should become clear to you as you continue to study.

We have one more important topic to consider in this part of Romans 6. Look at Romans 6:22 carefully and then compare it to Colossians 1:13 and Acts 26:18. What do these passages have in common?

Add the theme of Romans 6 to ROMANS AT A GLANCE.

DAY SEVEN

Store in your heart: Romans 6:23
Read and discuss: Romans 6

QUESTIONS FOR DISCUSSION OR INDIVIDUAL STUDY

- ∾ Read the first question Paul asks in Romans 6, and see if you can answer it from memory from what you studied.

- ∾ To be sure you have covered the main points, answer the following:

  1. What is our relationship to Christ?

  2. What is the purpose of our being raised from the dead?

  3. What happened to our old self?

  4. If our old self is dead, what is our new self?

  5. What is our relationship to sin now?

- ∾ What does Paul tell the Romans (and us) that they (and we) should do?

- ∾ What does "consider yourselves to be dead to sin, but alive to God in Christ Jesus" mean?

- ∾ What causes lusting in our mortal bodies? What are we not to let reign in our mortal bodies? How can you practically apply this to your life?

- ∾ What is an "instrument of unrighteousness"?

- ∾ Give examples of how you might use a part of your body as an instrument of righteousness.

∾ Is the physical body itself evil, or is our use of the body evil?

∾ Read the question in Romans 6:15 and explain how it relates to the question in Romans 6:1.

∾ Have you been freed from sin? Quote the verses in Romans 6 that help you answer.

∾ If you have been freed from sin (Romans 6:7), can you still act as if you were a slave to sin? What does Paul say in Romans 6 that helps you answer?

∾ Is sin the only thing you can be enslaved to?

∾ What is the result of enslavement to God?

∾ What are the wages of sin? What is the free gift of God?

THOUGHT FOR THE WEEK

Romans 6 is one of the most important chapters in the entire Bible for Christians to understand. It is a turning point in Paul's fundamental teaching about salvation by faith. Here we find the first exhortations or commands (the first practical applications) in the book of Romans, and they are related to the prior five chapters of pure doctrine.

Paul has spent considerable time and effort explaining that we are saved by grace, not works. God considers us righteous on the basis of our faith in Jesus' death for our sins and His resurrection to life. Sin kills. All mankind died because of Adam's sin, and sin has held mankind under its power and death sentence ever since. The Law came to point out sin—to show us God's standards—but it could not break the bonds of sin. It even made sin *increase* by aggravating man's natural rebellion against authority. It proved we needed something or someone to rescue us from sin's power.

Christ came in flesh, in our likeness, though without the sin of Adam. He was born "under the law" (He was born as a Jew after the Law came to lead us to Him), but he was perfectly obedient to the Law. He never committed sin, so His blood atoned for our sin. However, to defeat sin and death, He became sin for us (2 Corinthians 5:21) and died in our place. Christ's resurrection defeated sin and death, and it gives us freedom from death through faith. Our "old man" died with Christ. We now walk in newness of life.

We are a new creation, a *new man*, free from the bondage of sin. Sin is no longer our master. We have eternal life, so death no longer reigns over us. The new me, the person that I am, still lives in a mortal body, but the new me will live forever. When my body dies, the new me goes to be with the Lord. The new me is free from sin and death.

But the body I live in is not free from the presence of sin. Sin is like a computer's operating system in our physical bodies. My mouth is not sinful; I can use my mouth to serve sin or to serve righteousness. My brain and my mind are not sinful; I can use my mind to serve righteousness or unrighteousness. I am not free from the *presence* of sin, but rather I am free from the *power* of sin. This means sin does not have to reign in my life. I can now choose to sin or not sin.

That is the essential change. The gospel is the power of God for salvation. He has given me the power of the Holy Spirit as a gift. Because my old man in Adam is dead and the power of the Holy Spirit resides in me, I do not have to be a slave under sin. I have been set free; I just have to act like it. I must consider myself dead to sin and alive to Christ, and I must not let sin reign in my mortal body to obey its lusts. Sin is no longer my master, so I must not go on presenting the members of my body to it as instruments of unrighteousness as if it were still my master! How liberating is this truth? With this understanding we can live our lives with freedom—freedom in Christ!

We learned in the first five chapters that we are not justified by the Law, and in chapter 6 we see that we are not sanctified by the Law. I am saved *and* sanctified by grace. Nevertheless, I must act. We saw in Romans 6:19 that when we present ourselves as slaves to righteousness, the result is sanctification. I can obey, but only because God has given me His power in the Holy Spirit. I am no longer powerless to do right, enslaved to sin and death. I am finally free to live for my Good Master!

When I worked for the devil, I earned a fair wage. He paid me in the currency of his realm—death. But now I am free, and I live under God's grace. In my new freedom, shall I sin that grace may abound—that there would be more and more grace? Shall I sin because I am not under the Law? With great passion Paul says, "May it never be!"

The truth is, I am in Christ; I have been raised to newness of life in Him. I have been freed from sin and enslaved to God. Therefore, I must live like the person I am, not the person I was. God exhorts us through the apostle Paul to live for Him. Because God lives in me in the person of the Holy Spirit, I now can live for Him!

If I've been given all I need, how can I keep making excuses? How glorious it is to be set free and to be given power to live in freedom! But what will you do with that freedom, Beloved? Will you live any way you please, or will you diligently search the Scriptures to find what pleases God?

WHY THE LAW?

As you study Romans 7, we want to encourage you to let the Holy Spirit speak to your heart. You don't want to miss the rich message of this chapter—it's beautiful!

Paul has already affirmed that no man is justified by the Law. He teaches that instead, people are declared righteous through faith in the seed God promised to come through Abraham. The seed, we know from reading Galatians 3:16, is Jesus Christ. We saw that God justified Abraham *before* He gave the Law. Law brings sin to light, exposing it for what it is. We who have believed the promise are not under the Law, but under grace. What then are we to do with these truths about the Law? Is the Law sin? Did the Law cause my death? What is the purpose of the Law? If it couldn't justify us, can it sanctify us?

DAY ONE

Read and mark Romans 7:1-12 according to the bookmark you have been using. *Law* is used in different senses in this chapter (note the capitalization in the NASB). Watch for the difference as you mark.

DAY TWO

Read through Romans 7:1-6 again and think through the illustration of the married woman. When Paul gets to Romans 7:4-6, whom does he liken to the woman? Who or what does he liken to the Law? Who is likened to "another"? The woman is an adulterer if she is joined to another while still bound by the law (7:3) to her husband. But if he dies, she is free to join another.

It is so important, Beloved, that you don't miss the context of chapter 7. How does this relate to Romans 6? Who died in Romans 6? What are we freed from? Whom are we now joined to?

Label the parties Paul has mentioned.

the woman—

the husband—

another—

DAY THREE

You can help yourself follow Paul's train of thought throughout Romans by marking the questions he asks. Try just putting a big Q? in the margin. Now read Romans 7:7-12 and think through the second question. Is the Law sin? In your notebook, list what the Law did. Then list what sin did. What is the relationship between sin and the Law? You really need to write down these statements because they will appear clearer on paper. Take your time to reread and rehearse them until you can explain this relationship with confidence. Here are some helpful questions to use:

Before the Law, sin was what?

When the Law came, sin became what?

Before the Law, what did I know or not know?

When the Law came, sin did what?

So is the Law sin? Did the Law kill me? (Read Romans 7:13.)

DAY FOUR

Read and mark Romans 7:13-25 as you have been doing. Hang in there! Do not grow weary in doing well. Marking and observing carefully will bear much fruit. These chapters are deep and powerful, so taking your time is vital. You will be so glad you did!

DAY FIVE

Romans 7:13 asks another question. Let's focus on this important question and Paul's answer. In Romans 7:7, Paul asked whether the Law is sin. The answer, we have seen, is an emphatic *no*. Now Paul takes up the second question: Does the Law kill? The answer is clear in 7:13. No, sin kills, as Paul explains in Romans 7:14-25.

Read Romans 7:14 and note the contrast between the Law and sin. Read Romans 7:20. Where does Paul say sin dwells?

So what must be going on? Is something urging me to sin even though I am no longer a slave to sin? What did Paul say about this in Romans 7:7-11? So then, will keeping the Law make you more or less sinful?

That's enough for today. Let's rest our brains and take up the challenge again tomorrow. Hang in there!

DAY SIX

Read Romans 7:21-25. In your notebook, summarize the inner conflict between sin and law.

What does the Christian have that can overpower sin? What will set people free from the death that sin brings? I can't wait for chapter 8!

It's been a long day, but don't forget to summarize Romans 7 and add it to ROMANS AT A GLANCE.

DAY SEVEN

Store in your heart: Romans 7:6
Read and discuss: Romans 7:14-25

QUESTIONS FOR DISCUSSION OR INDIVIDUAL STUDY

- ∾ Review Romans 5:20-21; 6:6-9,12-14,17-18; 7:5-6.

- ∾ What seems to be the basic issue in Romans 7:14-25? What is the struggle we have in reconciling Romans 7:14-25 with Romans 5–6?

- ∾ Why did our old self die?

- ∾ What do we now have in us? What is the body's relationship to sin?

- ∾ Has the sin in us been rendered powerless? What are we to consider ourselves?

~ What does Romans 6:12-13,19 tell us we are to do? How do these verses relate to Romans 7:14-25?

~ How do we reconcile Romans 6:7,9,14 with Romans 7:14-25?

Thought for the Week

We aren't *justified* by the Law, and we aren't *sanctified* by the Law either. What could be clearer from Romans 7? Romans 6 explains that we died to sin, and in chapter 7 we learn that we died to the Law. We died to the Law so we might be joined to Christ. The Law only made sin alive. Paul shared that for him, the Law aroused coveting, which is sin, because it showed what coveting was.

Is the Law itself sin, or is it holy and righteous? No, it's not sin. Sin merely took opportunity through the Law, and sin deceived me and killed me just as surely as it did Adam and Eve in the Garden of Eden. Satan deceived Adam and Eve, and they sinned and died. The rest of the human race descended from Adam and Eve, so from Adam onward, death spread to all men. Sin was in the world, but when the Law came, it highlighted sin and showed man's inability to defeat sin.

But when the seed that God promised first to Eve and later to Abraham came and died, He rose from the dead, conquering sin and death and giving us the opportunity to bear fruit to God.

This is exciting and liberating news: We now have the Holy Spirit so we can live a new life by His power and not live in slavery to sin under the Law. With Paul, we can joyfully agree with the law of God in the inner man. We now eagerly want to serve God, and guess what—we have the power to do so!

This is possible only because the old man, who was enslaved to sin, was put to death in Christ. The new man rose in Christ and now rejoices because he was reconciled to God by the cross. We are "in Christ," which means we are no longer under the dominion of the old two masters—Satan and our own sin nature. We are free!

Our bodies still bear the marks of Adam, however. They are mortal; they are flesh. When we die, the body goes to the grave, but the spirit goes to be with God. The new self—the real me, which is reconciled to God and free from bondage to sin—goes to be with God. The body of flesh still bears the sting of death. It is corruptible and perishable. First Corinthians 15 describes the change that the body must undergo to be with God—from corruptible to incorruptible, from perishable to imperishable, from mortal to immortal. We shall be changed in the twinkling of an eye—glorified!

Galatians 5:17 teaches us that until then, our flesh is dead set against the Spirit: "For the flesh sets its desire against the Spirit, and the Spirit against the flesh; for these are in opposition to one another, so that you may not do the things that you please." The apostle John also mentioned our struggle with sin.

> If we say that we have no sin, we are deceiving ourselves and the truth is not in us. If we confess our sins, He is faithful and righteous to forgive us our sins and to cleanse us from all unrighteousness. If we say that we have not sinned, we make Him a liar and His word is not in us. My little children, I am writing these things to you so that you may not sin. And if anyone sins, we have an Advocate with the Father, Jesus Christ the righteous (1 John 1:8–2:1).

We who have believed are no longer slaves to sin; we now have the power to choose not to sin. Yet we have flesh to contend with—the force always pushing the members of our mortal body toward performing acts of sin. We are free from the *penalty* of sin (we have eternal life, not death), but we still have the *presence* of sin in our mortal bodies. Only when we receive glorified bodies are we free from the presence of sin. But here is the good news, Beloved: In the meantime, while living in this body, I do not have to obey the lusts of the flesh because I have been given the power of God to overcome that lust! I have a choice because I am free from sin's enslaving ownership.

Every day of my life, I must remind myself that I am a child of God and have God the Holy Spirit indwelling and empowering me to say no to sin and yes to God. *Every day* I must live in the truth that I *can* present the members of my body for righteousness because of this indwelling power of the Holy Spirit. *Every day* I must make it my will to live for God. I must choose to obey, to become more and more like Christ, to whom I have been joined. I must. I can. I will.

And so can you, Beloved. Everyone who has believed in Jesus has the Holy Spirit—you do, I do, we all do. And we all must make it our daily goal to live in that power and not make excuses as if we were helpless. We will learn more about this in the next chapter.

Too many who claim Christ as Savior also claim they are helpless. Are they helpless, powerless to escape continual sin? Are we? God says we're not. We have no excuse for living as if we can't help sinning. If you are a Christian, you are dead to sin and dead to the Law. So what's next? Keep reading!

LIVING BY THE SPIRIT

∾∾∾∾

Romans 8 begins with a blessed promise that can make us fall on our faces in humble gratitude: "There is therefore now no condemnation for those who are in Christ Jesus." From all that you have learned in the first half of Romans, this statement should come as a great comfort to your soul!

Romans 8 causes life and hope to course through our veins as we behold all that is ours because God's Spirit dwells within.

Romans 8 causes tears of joy to caress a beaming face as it closes with the promise that nothing can separate us from God's love because He is for us, Christ intercedes for us, and the Spirit emboldens us to cry, "Abba, Father."

DAY ONE

Before you begin, kneel before God the Father and ask Him, by His Spirit, to fulfill His promise to lead you into all the truth (John 16:13) as you study this invaluable chapter. Make sure your heart is right before God, your sins are confessed, you are walking in the light, and you have a completely teachable spirit before the Lord. Remember, when you cease to be teachable, your growth comes to a halt. All of us need to grow!

Now, read Romans 8:1-27, marking key words and phrases from your bookmark. Make any lists you think are critical to understanding this part of Romans 8. You will be amazed at how many times Paul refers to the Spirit.

DAY TWO

Now let's look at the principles in Romans 8:1-13. The most important lists in this section are about the Holy Spirit and the flesh. If you didn't make these lists, stop and do so. You don't want to miss the contrast between the two.

How does Romans 8 fit with Romans 7? What question did Paul ask in Romans 7:24? What verse in Romans 8 answers it? Go back and read Romans 6:5-6.

What did God do that the Law could not do? So what should we be doing now? How should we walk? How should we think? Where should our mind be set?

DAY THREE

Let's focus on Romans 8:14-17 today. According to Romans 8:9,14,16, what is the key test of whether we belong to Christ? If we pass this test, what is our relationship to the flesh? What does the Spirit do for us? What should we be doing by the Spirit?

These verses show us something new about who we are now that we are no longer slaves of sin. Paul explains that God has adopted us. As a result, we have two new identities. What are they?

Read Galatians 3:23–4:7; Ephesians 3:6; James 2:5. Notice the way these parallel what we have seen so far in Romans.

DAY FOUR

Today read Romans 8:18-27 again, and let's look at it in more detail. Notice the repetition of *groan* in these verses. Who groans and why? What is creation looking forward to? What do we look forward to? Review Genesis 3, especially verses 17-18.

When will this redemption of the body (Romans 8:23) come? Read 1 Corinthians 15:50-56. When will the earth escape its corruption? Read 2 Peter 3:7,10-13.

DAY FIVE

Read Romans 8:28-39, marking the items listed on your bookmark.

DAY SIX

Romans 8 includes some famous and powerful verses. I've underlined these in my Bible: 28,31,35,37-39. Why are these verses important to mark? Look at what they promise.

Let's not miss the important progression that occurs in Romans 8:28-30. List the progression.

God has predestined people to what? Why?

What can you list about the love of God?

These are powerful promises to remember. How do they relate to what we've seen so far in Romans? How secure is our relationship to Christ and to God the Father? And on whom does this relationship depend?

Add the theme of Romans 8 to ROMANS AT A GLANCE.

DAY SEVEN

Store in your heart: Romans 8:2 (and any other verses you desire—this chapter has several great ones!)

Read and discuss: Romans 8

QUESTIONS FOR DISCUSSION OR INDIVIDUAL STUDY

- What is the relationship of Romans 8:1-17 to Romans 6–7?

- What kind of life does God expect from those He has justified, those to whom He has given His Spirit?

- What point about the Law is reinforced by Romans 8:2?

- What is the connection between our corruption and the corruption of the world? What is the connection between the redemption of both? Can you tell?

- Who intercedes for us? How?

- Discuss the points in Romans 8:28-39 that show that God is for us.

- What promises in Romans 8 mean the most to you? How will you apply them to your life?

THOUGHT FOR THE WEEK

Free! Jesus proclaimed that if the Son makes you free, you will be free indeed (John 8:36). He was teaching about the same topic Paul addresses in Romans 8. Whoever commits sin is a slave of sin, but the Son sets you free from slavery to sin. And look at what Romans 8:2 says: "The law of the Spirit of life in Christ Jesus has set you free from the law of sin and death." Why? Because when you believed, you were given the Holy Spirit.

The reason God gave you the Holy Spirit is not so you can sit there and do nothing. According to Romans 8, we are to walk according to the Spirit and set our minds on the things of the Spirit. God will give us life through this Spirit who dwells in us. By the Spirit we put to death the deeds of the body, and by that Spirit we live. If we are led by the Spirit, we are sons of God.

Not only that, but the Spirit helps our weakness, interceding for us in prayer with groanings too deep for words.

How important is the indwelling Holy Spirit? Remember that when we say the Holy Spirit dwells in us, we are referring to God Himself. If we truly apprehend the idea of the Trinity, the triune, three-persons-in-one Godhead, we must come to grips with the fact that the Holy Spirit is just as much God as Jesus the Son and God the Father. *He* indwells us, not *it*.

God Himself tabernacled among Israel. His glorious cloud went before them and hovered over the mercy seat on the ark of the covenant in the holy of holies in the tabernacle and in the temple.

God Himself became flesh and dwelt among us in the person of Jesus of Nazareth, fully man and fully God. And He died for us, paying the debt we owed but could not pay. God the Father Himself loved us so much that He gave His only begotten Son to die for us.

And God the Holy Spirit Himself dwells in us. He doesn't hover at the end of the universe; He dwells in me and in you and in every person on the face of the earth who ever believed in God's promise.

He is the power that enables us to live. He is the power that enables us to set our mind on things above and not on the flesh. He is the power that enables us to say no to sin and yes to righteousness. And He who is in us intercedes for us in prayer, just as Jesus, who sits at the right hand of the Father, intercedes for us.

This indwelling Holy Spirit, God in us, is not with us in the sense of a companion. He is much more. He is not just "there for us," but is the active ingredient in good works—our power to do anything good. He is permanently in us. The love of God gave us His Son, Jesus, to die for us, but Jesus has returned to the Father. After He left, He sent the third person of the Godhead in His stead, the Spirit who dwells in us.

He does not come into us as He came upon Saul and David. He left Saul. He came upon David mightily, but today He *indwells* and *empowers* us. This is part of the promise of the new covenant that arrived with Jesus, long after Saul and David were gone. Ezekiel prophesied, "I will put My Spirit within you and cause you to walk in My statutes, and you will be careful to observe My ordinances" (Ezekiel 36:27).

Nothing will separate us from this permanent indwelling of the Spirit. That truth should make you rejoice, Beloved. We can be separated from anyone here on earth. We move away from friends and family and lose touch. Our lives get busy. Sometimes other circumstances get in the way and break up relationships. Sometimes our families are broken up by divorce. Sometimes death separates us. But nothing separates us from God's love or from His presence in us, the Holy Spirit. Regardless of what life's circumstances bring, we always have God in us. We are never, ever alone.

Perhaps you want to take a moment and meditate on that, Beloved. Think of the importance, the comfort of having One who never, ever leaves us.

Israel Did Not Pursue by Faith

Since Romans 1, Paul has been leading us up a steep and sometimes difficult ascent toward a pinnacle. As an eager but confident guide, he has urged us forward, for he wants to show us something vital, breathtaking, and magnificent. We must see it! Step by step, moment by moment, he has led us. As we have walked through Romans, we have been awed by the increasing beauty and scope of what we have seen in his gospel. Yet at times, we have become wearied along the way and asked, "Are you sure there is more to see? Have we not seen enough; is this view not sufficient? Are you sure it will help to climb higher?"

Nevertheless, Paul has urged us, exhausted and weary, to continue. Though we are convinced that we cannot take in any more, we have continued to climb. We're almost there—don't stop! You'll be sorry if you do, for if you stop here, you'll never see the complete scope of Paul's message, the magnificence of the gospel. Come higher, and you will see how completely it extends to Jew and Gentile. You'll see the culmination of this glorious gospel, and as you stand with us on the pinnacle, you will cry with us, "O God, from Thee, to Thee, and through Thee are all things. To Thee be the glory forever and ever. Amen!"

Paul has eloquently shown us that Jews and Gentiles are both saved by grace through faith and that the Law does not save or sanctify us. So a question arises: What about the Jew who has not believed? What will become of Israel?

DAY ONE

Remember that Paul wrote the book of Romans as a letter to a primarily Gentile church, yet that congregation of believers included a remnant of believing Jews who had recognized the Lord Jesus Christ as the long-awaited Messiah. But why were the Jews in the minority of believers when salvation was to come to and through their race? What had happened?

Read Romans 9, marking the key words as you have before.

DAY TWO

Read Romans 9 again and mark the following new key words for this segment: *covenant, choice (chosen),*[14] *Israel* (and pronouns), *saved,* and *mercy.* Add these to your bookmark.

DAY THREE

Just to be sure that we understand Paul in Romans 9–11, read Philippians 3:4-6 and list the items in Paul's description of himself.

Today, read Romans 9:1-13. In verse 3, what does Paul mean by "my kinsman according to the flesh"? According to Romans

9:4-5, what things belong to the Israelites? How do these three verses relate to each other? Why does Paul have great sorrow and grief for Israel? What has happened? Read John 1:11-12.

What point is Paul making with the Old Testament references to Isaac and Jacob? What key words let you know who the children of God are? If you are unfamiliar with the stories, read Genesis 17:1-19 and 25:21-26.

How would you summarize the principle in Romans 9:6-13?

DAY FOUR

Today, read Romans 9:14-18. What two aspects of God's character are discussed? How does Paul answer the charge that God is unjust?

An important principle to remember in Bible study is that Scripture interprets Scripture. We use this principle in cross-referencing passages in the Bible. Read 1 Timothy 1:12-16; Ephesians 2:4-9; 1 Peter 1:3. How has God shown mercy to us?

Read John 15:16; Romans 8:33; James 2:5; 1 Peter 1:1-2; 2 Peter 1:10. How does God's mercy relate to His choice? How does it relate to Jews and Gentiles?

DAY FIVE

In Romans 9:19, Paul anticipates an objection that God cannot find fault if no one can resist His will. This seems to make sense: If God sovereignly works in a man to will and to do sin, how can He fault him for it? How does Paul answer this objection in Romans 9:20-26?

Read Exodus 6:1-8. When did God choose Israel to be His people?

Romans 9:22-23 says God patiently endured vessels of wrath prepared for destruction to make known the riches of His glory upon vessels of mercy. Read Ephesians 2:10. Whom do you think Paul is referring to as vessels of wrath and vessels of mercy?

DAY SIX

The promise of a remnant is spread throughout Old Testament prophecies concerning Israel and Judah. One day, a remnant will inhabit the land. The subject is too broad for us to develop in this study, but consider these few select verses: Isaiah 10:20-22; Micah 7:18-20; Zephaniah 3:8-19; Zechariah 12:10; 13:6-9. How strong is the evidence in Scripture that a remnant of Israel will believe?

Why haven't they believed up to this point? Why have Gentiles been attaining righteousness, but Israel has not? Read Romans 9:30-33 to answer.

Record the theme of Romans 9 on ROMANS AT A GLANCE.

DAY SEVEN

 Store in your heart: Romans 9:31-32a

Read and discuss: Romans 9

QUESTIONS FOR DISCUSSION OR INDIVIDUAL STUDY

∾ What is Paul's great concern in Romans 9? What do you see about Paul's heart here?

∽ What attributes of God's character does Paul mention in his discussion of Israel in Romans 9?

∽ What did Israel rely upon to attain righteousness? How does this relate to all that Paul has discussed in Romans thus far about the Law and works?

∽ What are some wrong ways to pursue righteousness? What are some ways—other than believing the gospel—that *we* try to pursue righteousness?

∽ How did God act toward those who assumed that their lineage was their guarantee of righteousness? Will God still act this way today?

∽ Did God have a different plan of salvation for the Jews than He did for the Gentiles? What verses support your answer? Include references from chapter 4 if you have time.

∽ When did God prepare this plan? Did He make it up as He went along? What does this tell you about God's sovereignty?

THOUGHT FOR THE WEEK

Paul explained in great detail in Romans 1–5 that no one, Jew or Gentile, is excused before God. God has made Himself and His standard of righteousness known to all mankind. The Jews were entrusted with the oracles of God, but they pursued God by works, not by faith.

The Jews descended from Abraham, Isaac, and Jacob, the patriarchs to whom God gave the promises and covenants. Paul explains that God preached the gospel to Abraham: "The promises were spoken to Abraham and to his seed...that is, Christ" (Galatians 3:16). Abraham believed God, and it was counted to him as righteousness. The nation of Israel knew this because Moses wrote it all down in the Law.

The prophets kept telling the nation of Israel that it was going astray. They kept warning the people against works-based righteousness that falls short of God's mark. Yet few turned to God in faith. Still, God did not give up. He kept sending prophets who told of the Messiah to come. Finally, He sent His Messiah, but still Israel did not believe. For hundreds of years, the Gentiles had been excluded from God's election. They had no covenants with God, no worship system to point the way, no Law to be a tutor, no prophets to declare God's Word to them. Israel alone enjoyed this special privilege and love.

But God so loved the *world* that He sent His only begotten Son, Israel's promised Messiah, to bring eternal life to all men, not just to Israel. Israel had been given the responsibility of bringing the light of the special revelation God gave them to the dark world of the Gentiles. But they isolated themselves from Gentiles in their self-righteousness, calling them "dogs." Not until the Messiah came did the light spread to the Gentiles.

Paul had a great part in spreading that light—the light of Christ. It was his God-given stewardship. But Paul was a Jew too. His Jewish name was Saul. He was born into the tribe of Benjamin, circumcised on the eighth day, and trained in the Law by Gamaliel. He eventually became a Pharisee. As far as keeping the Law was concerned, he thought of himself as blameless.

But God chose Paul to be an instrument for the gospel—not to Jews, but to Gentiles. In this chapter, we see that Paul still loves his people. He has to explain what has happened and what will happen to Israel. He needs to explain it so that everyone will understand some vital characteristics of God—His sovereignty, His mercy, His choice, His faithfulness, His justice. He needs to be sure that the Jews do not draw wrong conclusions about their salvation.

He also wants to make sure Gentiles don't draw wrong conclusions about Israel from what they see. The Jews may not know the future God has in store, but God has revealed Israel's future to Paul. Though the nation rejected the righteousness that could come only by faith in the finished work of Jesus Christ, they are not cast off forever.

God does not save Jews one way and Gentiles another. All through this letter, Paul has shown that both Jew and Gentile are saved by faith. Both are under sin. Paul has used Abraham, circumcision, the Law, and David as powerful illustrations because the gospel reaches out to Jews as well as Gentiles. Paul himself is a Jew. Because faith is counted as righteousness, Abraham was saved. Because faith is counted as righteousness, David was saved. Because faith is counted as righteousness, Paul was saved. Because faith is counted as righteousness, Israel still has a chance.

Jews are not exempt from salvation by faith because of the Law. The Law was to show them the futility of law-keeping to overcome sin. Only faith in Messiah can lead to salvation, and until the day of His glorious return, the invitation remains open.

Righteousness does not depend on a certain number of days of good works, so the opportunity to believe extends to the day when Jesus returns. And so it is with Gentiles. Until the day a man draws his last breath, he has a chance. Even if one has continued to reject God before, he has hope if he will only believe. If we have the same love for our brethren according to the flesh that Paul had toward his, we too should grieve over our own kinsmen's unbelief. And we should trust in God's character as Paul did.

FAITH COMES BY HEARING

Romans 10 is really an extension of Romans 9. No distinction exists between Jew and Greek; the same Lord is Lord of all, abounding in riches for all who call on Him. Righteousness comes to both Jews and Greeks by faith, not works. The Law does not save. But this chapter emphasizes a different aspect of salvation by faith. Faith comes from hearing, and hearing by the word of Christ.

You're almost at the pinnacle! Why have you come this far? What motivated you to keep on climbing although the way has been steep, demanding, exhausting, difficult? We pray that someday God will look at you and say, "How beautiful are your feet" (see Romans 10:15).

DAY ONE

Read and mark Romans 10:1-13, using your bookmark as you have before. Don't miss mentions of the gospel. This chapter continues the segment that began in Romans 9.

DAY TWO

Paul has already laid the foundation that salvation is by faith, that it is a gift of grace and is not achieved by works of the Law. Romans 10:1-4 reinforces this idea. Read Romans 7:1-4 again and then Galatians 3:23-26 and Matthew 5:17. What point does Paul make in Romans 10:4?

Read Romans 10:8-10 again and mark every reference to *mouth* and *heart*. List what you learn from marking these words. Now go back and read Romans 3:10-20 and catch the contrast.

DAY THREE

Read and mark Romans 10:14-21 today, using your bookmark as usual.

DAY FOUR

Romans 10:14-15 is a series of questions, and we can see a progression by reversing the order. List the progression. First we need _____, then _____, and so on. Read Matthew 28:18-20. This passage in Matthew is universally called the Great Commission—the charge to the church to spread the good news of Jesus Christ to all nations. How does Romans 10 fit with Matthew 28:18-20?

The Greek word translated "preacher" means one who makes a public declaration. It is not a formal church office or position, though that is how people most often use the word today. A preacher is simply a herald—one who proclaims. Who qualifies to be a preacher of the gospel in this original sense?

DAY FIVE

What main point is made in Romans 10:16? Read Matthew 13:1-23 and mark every reference to *hear*.

DAY SIX

How does Romans 10:18-21 fit with verse 16? What aspect of hearing is addressed in verse 16? What aspect in verses 18-21?

What is Paul's point in quoting Moses and Isaiah in Romans 10:19-20? Reread the quote from Hosea in Romans 9:25.

Who is "a nation without understanding" (Romans 10:19)? Read 1 Peter 2:9-10; Revelation 5:9-10.

Add the theme of Romans 10 to ROMANS AT A GLANCE.

DAY SEVEN

 Store in your heart: Romans 10:9-10

Read and discuss: Romans 10:1-4,8-10,14-15,18-21

QUESTIONS FOR DISCUSSION OR INDIVIDUAL STUDY

- ∾ What basic desire does Paul express in chapter 10?

- ∾ Why hasn't all Israel been saved? Have some Jews become Christians? What did they do to be saved?

- ∾ What is the relationship between believing and confessing? What do you have to believe?

∾ What does Paul say about evangelism? What is needed?

∾ How do you feel when you share your faith with someone who does not respond? Do you get discouraged? How long has God been declaring the gospel?

∾ How could you respond when someone asks, "What about the people who have never heard the gospel?" (Hint: In addition to Romans 10, refer to Romans 1.)

∾ How strong is the evangelism program in your church? How strong is the evangelism program in your life? Will people hear if we don't tell them?

THOUGHT FOR THE WEEK

Last week we saw in chapter 9 that God is completely in control of man's salvation: "So then it does not depend on the man who wills or the man who runs, but on God who has mercy" (Romans 9:16). This week we saw man's role in salvation. "Faith comes from hearing, and hearing by the word of Christ" (Romans 10:17).

"How will they call on Him in whom they have not believed? How will they believe in Him whom they have not heard? And how will they hear without a preacher? How will they preach unless they are sent?" (Romans 10:14-15).

In the Great Commission, Jesus sent believers to all the nations to make disciples of all the peoples. Revelation tells us that Christ purchased men from every nation with His blood. God's plan of salvation was clearly not just for Israel but for all mankind. God intended Israel to be His agent to show Himself to the world. Part of Israel would produce the Messiah, whom God would make a light to all nations. In Isaiah 49:6, God says, "It is too small a thing that You should be My Servant to raise up the tribes of Jacob and to restore the preserved ones of Israel; I will also make You a light of the nations so that My salvation may reach to the end of the earth." God's plan goes beyond the borders of Israel!

So the good news must be proclaimed in all the earth. In Acts 1:8, Jesus says, "You shall be My witnesses both in Jerusalem, and in all Judea and Samaria, and even to the remotest part of the earth." The remainder of the book of Acts is a record of the obedience of these first Jewish believers to the Great Commission. In Acts 8, the disciples are scattered in Judea and in Samaria, where Philip is preaching. Later, Philip finds an Ethiopian eunuch on the road from Jerusalem to Gaza (in Judea) and preaches the gospel to him. Saul encounters Christ on the road to Damascus and then travels throughout the eastern Mediterranean, in what is today Turkey, Cyprus, and Greece. The word has already spread to Rome by the time he writes.

God's people were being faithful to the charge Jesus gave them. Today, people are taking the gospel to nations in the remotest parts of the earth, laboring to translate the Bible into their languages.

But what about our next-door neighbors? How will they call on Him in whom they have not believed, and how will they believe if no one shares the good news with them? We shouldn't shuck our responsibility and hope missionaries from Guatemala will show up on their doorsteps. The responsibility—or better yet, the privilege—to share the good news is ours!

The unbelieving Jew has the Old Testament Law, but he doesn't know how to conform to it the way God requires (Deuteronomy 28:1). Rejecting the One who fulfilled the righteous requirements of the Law and satisfied its penalties in our place, he seeks self-righteousness. But without the Spirit of God indwelling and empowering, fulfilling God's Law is impossible.

And the Spirit indwells and empowers only those who place their faith in the life and death of Jesus Christ.

God has intended for the Gentile to make the Jew jealous by *receiving through faith* what the Jew *seeks by works*—righteousness before God. This is opposed to every kind of self-righteousness. This specific faith comes only by hearing, and hearing comes only by the word of Christ.

Even though the following exercise may seem awkward to you, repeat the statement below out loud, stressing the words we've put in italics. Ask God to speak something new to you through it, and ask yourself how each version is meaningful and applicable to your life. See if you know a scripture to support each stressed term:

We must proclaim Christ to our neighbors.

We *must* proclaim Christ to our neighbors.

We must *proclaim* Christ to our neighbors.

We must proclaim *Christ* to our neighbors.

We must proclaim Christ *to* our neighbors.

We must proclaim Christ to *our* neighbors.

We must proclaim Christ to our *neighbors.*

"How beautiful are the feet of those who bring good news of good things!" (Romans 10:15)

Acts 4:12 tells us, "There is salvation in no one else; for there is no other name under heaven that has been given among men by which we must be saved." No one can proclaim this except those who know it and have believed. But they can be confident because the fields are white for harvest. Remember Romans 10:9-10: "If you confess with your mouth Jesus as Lord, and believe in your heart that God raised Him from the dead, you will be saved; for with the heart a person believes, resulting in righteousness, and with the mouth he confesses, resulting in salvation."

What will you do, Beloved? Will you someday hear God say, "How beautiful are your feet!"

HAS GOD REJECTED ISRAEL?

Can you imagine Paul standing on the pinnacle, reaching down with outstretched hands, waiting to grasp the somewhat shaky hand reaching up to his, and smiling as he hears, "But Paul, tell me…I must know—God hasn't rejected Israel, has He? I know that for so long He has stretched out His hand to a disobedient people, even as you stretched out yours to mine. Has God given up? Will Israel never be saved? Oh, it is so hard to understand! Sometimes I can't straighten it all out in my mind and make the pieces fit together!"

And can you imagine his response? "Come on, grasp my hand, and I will lead you to the top. We can sit under a beautiful olive tree, and I will explain it all to you."

May God open the eyes of your understanding so that you might believe even that which is beyond your knowledge or wisdom, accepting it by faith because it is the word of the Lord. May God grant us His revelation!

DAY ONE

Romans 11 is the final chapter in this third segment, which focuses on the sovereignty of God in salvation. It also concludes

97

the doctrinal teaching that Paul so very skillfully lays out in Romans 1–11.

Pay careful attention to the questions Paul anticipates and his answers as you read Romans 11:1-16, marking as you have before. The word *remnant* is key in this chapter, although it is used only once. You might mark it like this: remnant. It is also used in Romans 9:27. Go back and mark it there.

DAY TWO

Read Romans 11:1-16 again and answer these questions:

1. How does Paul answer the question he asks in Romans 11:1? How does his being an Israelite prove that God has not rejected Israel?

2. Who makes up this remnant that will be saved?

3. Why weren't they saved earlier?

4. What was the purpose of their stumbling? Who benefits?

5. Who is Paul an apostle to? Why does Paul's Jewish heritage make him a suitable apostle to the Gentiles? Why not choose a Gentile to do this?

6. How is Romans 11:1-16 consistent with Romans 1–10? In other words, what key doctrines about God and salvation are repeated here?

DAY THREE

Read and mark Romans 11:17-36. Don't miss *saved* and *covenant*.

DAY FOUR

Romans 11:16 transitions us to some metaphors. The first metaphor is a lump of dough. Paul says if a piece broken off from this lump is holy, the entire lump is. Leaven is used in Scripture to represent pervasive growth—either of the kingdom of heaven (Matthew 13:33) or of sin (1 Corinthians 5:6-8). Which kind of leavening do you suppose Paul has in mind in Romans 11:16?

The second metaphor—the root and the branches (Romans 11:16)—is clear because it obviously parallels the previous one of the lump of dough and a piece broken off. This metaphor is expanded in verses 17-24. Read these verses carefully and answer the following:

1. Who is the natural olive tree?

2. What is meant by "the root is holy"?

3. Who are the branches from the olive tree that were cut off?

4. Who is the wild olive tree?

5. What were the branches from the wild olive tree grafted into?

6. What are the natural branches that are grafted back into their own olive tree?

7. What does this metaphor teach us doctrinally?

DAY FIVE

Now read Romans 11:25-32 again. The phrase "fullness of the Gentiles" speaks of the culmination of a period when God is primarily saving Gentiles, after which His Son returns to rebuild the tabernacle of David that has fallen (Amos 9:11; Acts 15:16; Romans 11:26). This period is the "times of the Gentiles" (Luke 21:24).

List what you see about the Deliverer and what happens when He comes. Who is the Deliverer, and when will He come? Now answer the following:

- ∞ When will Israel be saved with respect to the Gentiles? With respect to the Deliverer?

- ∞ What does Paul say about God's choice?

- ∞ About God's gifts?

- ∞ About God's calling?

What does Romans 11:30-32 reveal about God's mercy and the way it relates to the Gentile, the Jew, and you?

DAY SIX

Now read Romans 11:33-36. This is a wonderful doxology— a hymn that contains an ascription of praise to God. You may be familiar with the doxology "Praise God from Whom All Blessings Flow," which is often sung during offerings in church worship services. Create a list of Paul's valuations of God in this doxology (Romans 11:33-36).

In what ways is this a fitting end to this three-chapter segment on the sovereignty of God?

In what ways is this a fitting end to Romans 1–11? Consider the majesty of God's character and of the salvation that Paul has been teaching about in these 11 chapters.

If you're not too embarrassed, you might consider breaking out in a praise song yourself. Does any tune come to mind?

Record the theme of Romans 11 and any segment divisions on ROMANS AT A GLANCE.

DAY SEVEN

Store in your heart: Romans 11:25b-26
Read and discuss: Romans 11:11-32

Questions for Discussion or Individual Study

- Discuss the details of the metaphor of the olive tree and branches. Review the details you observed in this metaphor before discussing their meaning.

- Who is the natural olive tree? Who is the wild olive tree? Who is the root?

- What has happened to some branches of the natural olive tree?

- What has happened to some branches from the wild olive tree?

- Do the branches from the natural olive tree have any hope?

- How is this metaphor explained by Romans 11:25?

- How does Romans 11:26-27 explain when this will occur?

- What is Israel's standing before God?

- Discuss what you learn about God from these verses.

THOUGHT FOR THE WEEK

Always remember that God is not finished with Israel. He has not rejected His people. A partial hardening has happened until the fullness of the Gentiles has come in, and then all Israel will be saved.

What has God laid on your heart, Beloved, toward the Jew? What should be your attitude toward the Jew? What should you pray for, work for, and hope for with respect to individual Jews—in your community, in your country, and in all the world—and the nation of Israel?

Why don't you ask God to show you what you can do to have beautiful feet?

Remember, understanding God's character is key to understanding His ways. God never acts in a way that is contradictory to His character. God is faithful. He is a covenant-keeping God, so when He makes a promise, He keeps it. Therefore, the gifts and calling of God are irrevocable.

Based on this last statement, think about how secure your salvation is. Who called you, and how did you get salvation according to Romans 5:15-17?

Understanding that our salvation is neither achieved by works nor kept by works is absolutely critical. We are free from the Law. The Law does not justify or sanctify us; God does. God's sovereignty is sure from foreknowledge to glorification, from start to finish and in between—this is what we need to remember from Romans 6–8. God the Holy Spirit secures our sanctification by coming to dwell in us so that we have the power to make right choices. When we are transferred from sin's ownership to God's, from slavery to freedom, from Satan's kingdom to the kingdom of God's beloved Son, we are not left alone. God Himself is in us.

Paul intimates that we may not fully understand why God does what He does: "Who has known the mind of the Lord?"

God certainly doesn't owe us explanations: "Who has first given to Him that it might be paid back to him again?" While we were yet sinners, Christ died for us. He sovereignly chose us. As Romans 8:29-30 summarizes,

> Those whom He foreknew, He also predestined to become conformed to the image of His Son, so that He would be the firstborn among many brethren; and these whom He predestined, He also called; and these whom He called, He also justified; and these whom He justified, He also glorified.

Surely this is the Bible's clearest statement of the sovereignty of God in our salvation. Look at the words in the middle of those two verses: "predestined to become conformed to the image of His Son." God's intent is for us to be conformed to the image of His Son. And that's exactly what Paul addresses next in this great letter. After eleven chapters of doctrine, the last five chapters are pure application—what we should do to carry out the command of Romans 6 as we're conformed to the image of the Son of God.

We must consider ourselves dead to sin and alive to Christ. We must not let sin reign in our mortal bodies to obey its lusts or present the members of our bodies to sin as instruments of unrighteousness. Rather, we must present ourselves to God as alive from the dead and present our members as instruments of righteousness to God. We must do this because of what God has done for us, is doing for us, and will do for us in Christ Jesus through the Holy Spirit.

We don't walk according to the flesh, but according to the Spirit. We are in Christ, free from sin, and enslaved to God.

And all of this is true for Jew and Gentile alike. The wild olive branch is grafted into the natural olive tree! Remember this as you carry the good news with beautiful feet!

PRESENT YOUR BODIES
A LIVING SACRIFICE

How then shall we live? How should the magnificent doctrinal foundation Paul has laid in the previous 11 chapters affect my daily activities? Paul gives us answers in these last five chapters, the final segment of Romans, as he shifts from doctrine to practice. These final chapters are all application, for there is no room in the body of Christ for a bunch of know-it-all doctrinal gurus—we need to be living according to sound doctrine. It's not enough, Beloved, to know the truth. We need to know what God expects from our behavior, and we need to obey Him.

There is also a good lesson to be learned in his structure of the book. Truth comes first and then practice. We must learn God's Word before we apply it to our lives. Also notice the weight given to each part. Eleven chapters are devoted to doctrine and five chapters to application.

Chapter 12 begins with a command to present our bodies as a living sacrifice to God. The rest of Romans 12–16 tells us how to do just that.

We're going to pick up the pace over these last chapters, finishing all five chapters in just two weeks, because their content is easier to digest. Hang in there and don't give up because they're packed with practical wisdom that we need to live by.

DAY ONE

Read Romans 12, marking as you have before. In this new segment, we'll be adding some new words to your bookmark. Here in Romans 12, add *love*, which you can mark with a red heart shaded red inside.

DAY TWO

This is a powerful chapter with a powerful opening. Paul urges his Roman brethren to continually present their bodies a living and holy sacrifice. This is the great *therefore*, following 11 chapters of the doctrine of righteousness by faith.

Write the two things from verse 2 that we are to do as part of this living sacrifice.

Conformed has to do with externals—what we look like to others. Your garden, for example, can be conformed to an English or Dutch garden with different kinds of plants and arrangements. *Transformed* has to do with the inner man. A parking lot can be transformed into a garden.

What is the vehicle for transformation? How has the book of Romans helped you to be transformed?

Make a list of behaviors that Paul urges from Romans 12:3-13.

How does Romans 12:4-8 help us understand Romans 12:3?

If you have time, read 1 Corinthians 12; Ephesians 4:8-12; 1 Peter 4:10-11. The subject of spiritual gifts is too broad to study in depth here, but these cross-references are the other places where the subject is discussed in detail.

Romans 12:9 takes up the subject of love. How does Romans 12:11-13 help explain verse 10?

How does Romans 12:10 relate to verse 3?

DAY THREE

List the actions Paul urges in Romans 12:14-21.

Do you think these behaviors should be directed only to people in the body of Christ or to everyone?

How does Romans 12:16 relate to verse 3 and verse 10?

Read Romans 12:19-21 again. What in verses 20-21 explains verse 19?

In the context of overcoming evil with good—feeding your enemy, giving him a drink, and not taking revenge—what did Paul mean by "in so doing you will heap burning coals on his head"? Is this result good or evil? (Interpretations abound. What do you think from the context?)

Record the theme of Romans 12 on ROMANS AT A GLANCE.

DAY FOUR

Read Romans 13, marking as you have done before. For this chapter, add *authority*[15] *(authorities)* and *minister.*[16] Choose new symbols and colors for these.

DAY FIVE

List everything you learn about authorities from Romans 13:1-7. What should our relationship to authorities be? Why?

What functions do authorities perform with respect to those who do evil? Those who do good?

Is there any hint that believers should relate one way to good authorities and another way to bad ones? Who gives good rulers authority? Who gives bad rulers authority?

Read 1 Timothy 2:1-4; Titus 3:1; 1 Peter 2:13-16.

The Greek word that the NASB translates as *tax* (KJV and NIV: *tribute*) referred to the tribute a conquered nation paid to a conqueror. If Rome conquered your nation, you were required to pay the Roman tribute. The word translated *custom* (ESV, NIV: *revenue*) denotes a tax on goods, like the duties you pay on your return to your country for items you purchased in a foreign country.

Read Luke 20:22-25. What is the Christian's appropriate attitude regarding taxes?

DAY SIX

Read Romans 13:8-10 and list what you learn about *love*. Then read Matthew 5:17; John 13:34-35; 15:12; 1 John 3:10; 4:7-12. What is the New Testament teaching about loving one another?

Read Romans 13:11-14 and then Matthew 5:14-16. What do we learn about darkness and light?

Read Romans 6:4; 8:4 about how we should walk. Then read 2 Corinthians 5:7; Galatians 5:14-25; Ephesians 5:8-14. How do loving one another and walking in the light go together?

Finally, record the theme of Romans 13 on ROMANS AT A GLANCE.

DAY SEVEN

Store in your heart: Romans 12:1-2

Read and discuss: Romans 12:1-3,10-19; 13:1-10

QUESTIONS FOR DISCUSSION OR INDIVIDUAL STUDY

- What does presenting a living sacrifice (rather than a dead one) mean? What was done in the Old Testament, and how does this differ from presenting a living sacrifice? What should our motivation be?

- What is our relationship to the world to be like? Discuss practical examples of how our behavior might "be conformed to this world."

- Discuss how transformation takes place according to Romans 12:2. What changes do we need to make in our lives to be obedient to this?

- What kind of attitude toward others *should* we have according to Romans 12:3,10,16? What kind of attitude toward others *do* we often have? Do any attitudes in your life need transforming?

- What is the right attitude toward our enemies— those who persecute us or do bad things to us? How can we practically obey Romans 12:19-21?

- Discuss the proper relationship between governing authorities and God.

- Discuss the proper relationship between governing authorities and the Christian. Have you always had the right relationship with a president, governor, senator, congressman, mayor, city councilman, or other government official, especially one with whom you disagreed? Would you like to change anything in yourself?

ఐ How does this relate to taxes? Does a tax irritate you? Does the principle of paying taxes, the amount you pay, or the way other people use your hard-earned money bother you? Do you need to make any adjustments in your relationships with governing authorities?

ఐ Will you walk in the light? Will you let your light shine? Will you walk in the Spirit?

Thought for the Week

What is a living and holy sacrifice? In the Old Testament, Israelites brought sacrificial offerings to the priest at the altar in the tabernacle or temple. They would kill the animal and burn it on the altar. The animal had to be unblemished—holy—to be dedicated to the Lord. The high priest's turban was adorned with the words "Holy to the LORD" (Exodus 28:36-37).

The animal qualified for sacrifice if it was of high value and not cast-off, secondhand, blemished, unusable, or unsellable. (God made provision for poor people who didn't have an animal to sacrifice and couldn't afford to buy one. See Leviticus 5:7,11; 12:8; Luke 2:24.) The prophet Malachi railed against Israel because the people were insulting God with lame and sick animals they wouldn't offer to a local governor, let alone a king. God said that such actions profaned His name and that such people were no more than swindlers trying to get His favor in spite of giving Him less than He was due.

God asks us to sacrifice. We must give up something valuable. God has given us His Son; what sacrifice can we make in return? He asks for our freedom. He asks us to place our devotion to ourselves and our pleasures on His altar as a living sacrifice. He does not ask us to literally kill ourselves; rather, He asks us to consecrate our bodies to His glory. We are to figuratively lay our lives on the altar, having died with Christ, died to sin, and died to the Law but being alive to God in Christ Jesus. Our bodies are to be holy to the Lord. Paul calls this action our "spiritual service of worship."

As living sacrifices we must not be conformed to this world or age—to its ideas, morals, attitudes, and behaviors. We must not look like the world in speech, dress, or behavior. What does this mean? We have already seen many passages about living in or walking by the Spirit rather than the flesh. Ephesians 4 tells us we are to lay aside the behaviors of the old self and be renewed in the spirit of our mind.

We must learn what the Word of God says about the deeds of the flesh and the fruit of the Spirit. We must direct our mind to dwell on things God says are worthy of praise (Philippians 4:8). We must choose to be changed from the inside by the renewing of our mind so that our outside doesn't look like the world.

This kind of change—not superficial but real and deep—enables us to test what the will of God is. Without a substantial change, we are unable to see as God sees and truly discern His will. We can confuse it with worldly ideas because we are not looking through God's eyes, seeing as He sees. God's will is good and acceptable and perfect; our will can be everything but unless we are transformed by the renewing of our mind.

Only then can we decide rightly to do what God desires. Then we have presented our bodies as a living and holy sacrifice, acceptable to God. *Only then* can we think of others before ourselves. *Only then* can we love without hypocrisy, abhor evil, and cling to good. *Only then* can we relate to our enemies in Christlike behavior and be at peace with all men, so far as it depends on us. *Only then* can we relate to governing authorities as God would have us, even when they are evil, when they do things contrary to the Word of God. Then we can pay taxes in good conscience, though we may disagree with the amounts or uses of them. Then we can love one another and fulfill the law.

Then we will be letting our light shine as Jesus taught in the Sermon on the Mount. We will spread light throughout the darkness of the world, dispelling darkness by the light of Christ shining through us. And then will the world be able to see, having rejected the knowledge of God in creation and having been given over to depraved minds. When we shine in this dark world, people may open their eyes and turn from darkness to light and from the dominion of Satan to God to receive forgiveness of sins and an inheritance among those who have been sanctified by faith in God.

So, how's your love life, Beloved? Does it draw from a well-spring of living water that will never, ever fail? Are you tapped into the Source of love? Is love flowing from you so that all may taste the sweetness?

Remember, whether someone drinks the living water or is satisfied is not your responsibility. All that is yours to do is to love with the love of Christ so that others may see what the love of the Father is all about and discover the Source of the living water that flows out of you.

BEAR THE WEAKNESSES OF THOSE WITHOUT STRENGTH

Did you come to the altar of sacrifice? Then like us, you are His to do His will, and we are all in the process of being transformed by the renewing of our minds. How blessed we are to know the truth and by that truth to be set free. May God greatly use these chapters to renew our minds that we might be transformed, enabling us to walk according to our liberty, His love, and Christ's example.

DAY ONE

Before you begin, tell God that you want His truth above all else, even if knowing His truth means you must admit that you have been wrong about certain things, and even if walking in His truth means that you must go to others and confess to them that you have been wrong. Without a teachable heart, a humble spirit, and an obedient will, you will never grow.

Now read Romans 14, marking key words as you have before. Add *weak(ness)* and *brother* to your bookmark. Be sure to mark synonyms. *Judge(judgment)* should already be on your bookmark from Romans 1–5. It appears again several times here in Romans 14.

DAY TWO

Read 1 Corinthians 8. Then from Romans 14 and 15 and 1 Corinthians 8, list what you learn about the weak brother. What is his motivation? Is his motivation right?

How then are we to relate to our weaker brother? Why? What does putting an obstacle or stumbling block in a brother's way mean? If we hurt a brother, what are we no longer walking in?

What is key about Romans 14:23? How does this relate to what Paul has said about faith in the previous 13 chapters?

Record the theme of Romans 14 on ROMANS AT A GLANCE.

DAY THREE

Read and mark Romans 15. We've put every key word we'll need on the bookmark by now. *Gentiles* appears again in this chapter, as well as many references to *Paul*.

DAY FOUR

Romans 15 continues the teaching from Romans 14 about weak believers. You may want to add to what you learned in Romans 14 about how we are to relate to the weaker brother. What motivation does Paul use in Romans 15?

List how Christ acted—He's the example Paul calls us to follow.

How does Paul tie the idea of Jew and Gentile into this discussion?

We looked at Romans 15:15-32 in week 1, so we don't need to dwell there, but read it again and notice the use of the key word *gospel*. What is always Paul's ultimate motivation and goal?

Record the theme of Romans 15 on ROMANS AT A GLANCE.

DAY FIVE

Read Romans 16 today. This chapter doesn't contain much to mark because it is mostly Paul's greetings to Christian friends. However, you will notice their relationship to Christ and to Paul. Notice how Paul expects them to greet one another. Some people have a hard time hugging—can you imagine if your pastor asked you this Sunday to greet one another with a holy kiss? Now *that* would be fellowship in a whole new manner!

Have you ever thought about how we express love in our natural families? If we love one another in the body of Christ, how should we express love in this family?

Romans 16:17-19 contains a command from Paul to the Romans that bears application for today too. Don't miss the main point.

When you're done, add the theme of Romans 16 to ROMANS AT A GLANCE.

DAY SIX

You made it! We have come to the end of our study. By now ROMANS AT A GLANCE has all 16 chapter themes on it. You can add all the key words you marked and anything else you have discerned. Lastly, write the theme of Romans on the chart. Perhaps you can select a key verse or phrase, something Paul emphasizes over and over, that sums up the message of Romans. If so, use that. Chapter or book themes are not inspired because God didn't write any in His Word. But since you've studied so diligently, you should be able to discern a good summary. The secret is to think about which key words and ideas permeate the book. What does Paul emphasize the most by repeating?

Review all of Romans. Just sit down and read through all 16 chapters and then spend some time in reflection on what you learned. Could you tell someone the main segments of Romans? Which chapters cover which subjects? Knowing Romans will be so vital to your walk, and it will help you understand many other things in Scripture.

If one of us could see you in person, we would show you some body language to help you remember Romans. For example, Romans 1:1–3:20 covers *sin*. Hold your upper arm vertically and use your hand to imitate a snake's head, like a cobra, because the snake reminds us of the serpent who introduced sin into the world.

Romans 3:21–5:21 is about *salvation*—justification by faith in Christ's finished work on the cross. Put your arms out to the side so your body and arms made a cross, and bow your head as Christ did on that cross. God saves us through His Son. We are saved by grace.

Romans 6–8 is about *sanctification*, so use one hand to make a halo over your head, since the same word is used for *sanctified* and *holy*. We are sanctified by the Holy Spirit.

Romans 9–11 is about God's *sovereignty* in allowing Israel to be hardened that the Gentiles might be grafted into the olive tree. God is sovereign in salvation. Fold your arms over each other and then with one arm act like a judge banging a gavel.

Romans 12–16 is application of Paul's teaching to your life of *service* to God because He has saved you from sin and sanctified you by His grace, sovereignly grafting you into one tree. Make a motion as if you're serving a tennis ball.

Sin, salvation, sanctification, sovereignty, service. It even alliterates! Practice this until you can recite it to someone; then you'll know you've gotten it. Perhaps you would like to spend some time in prayer or praise to God for His grace.

DAY SEVEN

 Store in your heart: Romans 14:23
Read and discuss: Romans 14:1–15:6

QUESTIONS FOR DISCUSSION OR INDIVIDUAL STUDY

- What does Paul mean by "weak in faith"?

- What should be the attitude of the strong toward the weak? The weak toward the strong?

- To whom are we accountable for our actions?

- What stumbling blocks do we put before brothers or sisters in Christ?

- How does this discussion of not hurting a brother relate to Romans 13 and Paul's teaching about love?

- What can you think of besides food and drink that can be stumbling blocks? What other convictions do Christians have about behavior that is pleasing to God?

- What do you think you will do when you see someone who appears weak in faith?

- If you have any time left, wrap up your study by

sharing verses from Romans that spoke deeply to your hearts, ones you know you'll remember.

THOUGHT FOR THE WEEK

It seems hard to believe that we have spent three months studying Romans. What a fabulous book! Perhaps now you can see why some call it "The Constitution of Our Faith." So many great theological ideas and doctrines are carefully laid out. We've seen the depravity of man: Jew and Gentile are sinners; none is righteous. All have sinned and fallen short of the glory of God.

We've seen how sin and death entered the world through Adam—the doctrine of original sin. We've seen how justification is credited to our account by God's grace through faith in Christ alone. And we've seen propitiation—Christ's satisfaction of the debt we owed for sin. We no longer have to pay the penalty for sin.

We've seen redemption. Christ redeemed us from sin, and we are set free from the Law and sin. We've seen that we are not only justified but also sanctified by grace through the power of the Holy Spirit, who dwells in us. We are no longer bound by sin's power, though we are not yet free from sin's presence.

We've also seen the sovereignty of God in salvation, and the gospel as the power of God for salvation for the Jew first and then the Greek. We've seen how the Jew and Gentile are used together in God's plan of salvation for the world and that grace is the only reason Gentiles have been given the privilege of being adopted into the family of God, grafted as wild branches into the olive tree whose root is holy—Jew and Gentile in one body.

And we are granted the privilege of serving God. After understanding this compendium of doctrinal truth, God expects us to present ourselves a living and holy sacrifice. We are urged not to be conformed to the world but to be transformed by the renewing of our mind, to prove the will of God, and to do what is good, acceptable, and perfect.

Our prayer is that your mind will be renewed by the Word of God, that you will be *transformed*—that you will undergo metamorphosis instead of continuing to be *conformed* to the world.

If one key word sticks out in this great book of Romans, it's *faith*. Near the beginning of this letter, Paul writes, "The righteous shall live by faith." Near the end, he says, "Whatever is not of faith is sin." The point of the book is that even though we were once sin's slaves, we have now been set free by redemption. Our justification was credited to us when we believed Christ's gospel. *Free* means we are no longer to live as slaves. We are to understand the truth of *righteousness by faith alone in Christ alone* and no longer live under sin's sway. We are not slaves, so we are not to live as slaves. We do not have to sin; we have power in the Holy Spirit to say no to sin and yes to God. We must grow in likeness to Christ by yielding ourselves to the Holy Spirit, remembering who we are and not allowing Satan to trick us into saying yes to sin. We need not give in to lusts of the eyes and flesh or to pride. Because of Jesus, we are worthy to be called children of God.

We should walk in the light, walk as we really are, presenting ourselves a living and holy sacrifice to God. We should be examples to all mankind, declaring by words and deeds God's grace, mercy, and peace to the whole world.

"Now may the God of hope fill you with all joy and peace in believing, so that you will abound in hope by the power of the Holy Spirit" (Romans 15:13).

But most of all, Beloved, let us not forget that in our knowledge of doctrinal truth we have a great responsibility not only to teach truth but also to live it. What a force the church of Jesus Christ could be if its members would stop tearing down one another over nonessential practices, about which God's Word has remained silent! How dare we add legalistic burdens that He never placed there! How dare we judge one another's spirituality by a measure God never laid out in His Word! How dare we look down with contempt at a brother whose conscience will not permit him to do the things we feel free to do! How dare we play God, reject one another, and blind the world to Christ!

Live in light of the truth of God. But live in love. Proclaim the truth of the Word of God, in season and out; use it to reprove, to correct, to teach, but always in the love of God and for the reasons that God gave us truth. Be a force in the world for truth, God's truth, but be a force in the world for love, God's love, that all men might know Christ and be drawn to Him.

ROMANS AT A GLANCE

Theme of Romans:

SEGMENT DIVISIONS

				CHAPTER THEMES
				1
				2
				3
				4
				5
				6
				7
				8
				9
				10
				11
				12
				13
				14
				15
				16

Author:

Date:

Purpose:

Key Words:

Notes

1. KJV: *vengeance* in Romans 3:5
2. KJV, NKJV: *changed*
3. ESV, KJV, NKJV: *God gave them up*
4. ESV: also *judges, condemn*; KJV, NKJV: *condemnation*; NIV: *condemn, condemned, condemnation*
5. ESV: *By no means!*; KJV: *God forbid*; NKJV: *Certainly not!*; NIV: *Not at all!*
6. ESV: *counted*; KJV: *counted, reckoned, impute(d,th)*; NKJV: *accounted, counted, impute(d)*
7. KJV, NKJV: *glory*; ESV, NIV: *rejoice*
8. KJV: *glory*; NIV: *brag*
9. ESV, KJV, NKJV: *dominion*
10. ESV: also *enslaved*; KJV: *serve, servants, bondage*
11. KJV, NKJV: *old man*
12. NIV: *parts*
13. KJV, NKJV: *reckon*; NIV: *count*
14. ESV, KJV, NKJV, NIV: *elect(ion)*
15. ESV: also *authorities*; KJV: *power (powers)*
16. ESV, NIV: *servant*

Books in the
New Inductive Study Series

❧❧❧❧

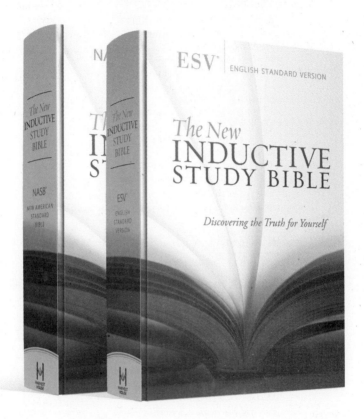

HARVEST HOUSE BOOKS BY KAY ARTHUR

Discover 4 Yourself® Inductive Bible Studies for Kids

Do you want a life that thrives?

Wherever you are on your spiritual journey, there is a way to discover Truth for yourself so you can find the abundant life in Christ.

Kay Arthur and Pete De Lacy invite you to join them on the ultimate journey. Learn to live life God's way by knowing Him through His Word.

Visit www.precept.org/thrives to take the next step by downloading a free study tool.